COLONEL AARON BURR

The American Phoenix

By Samuel Engle Burr, Jr.

HISTORICAL AND BIOGRAPHICAL

Small-Town Merchant
Colonel Aaron Burr: The American Phoenix

EDUCATION

An Introduction to Progressive Education
A School in Transition
An Introduction to College

GOVERNMENT AND CITIZENSHIP

Our Flag and Our Schools
A Handbook on the Government of the United States

TRAVEL AND ADVENTURE

China A.P.O.: More Than Experience

COLONEL AARON BURR

The American Phoenix

A Study of
His Life and Career

by

Samuel Engle Burr, Jr.

An Exposition–Lochinvar Book

EXPOSITION PRESS   NEW YORK

EXPOSITION PRESS INC., 386 Park Avenue So., New York 16, N.Y.

SECOND, REVISED EDITION

EP 42019

To the memory of
Colonel Burr's mother
ESTHER EDWARDS BURR
his sister
SARAH BURR REEVE
his wife
THEODOSIA BARTOW BURR
and his daughter
THEODOSIA BURR ALSTON

Acknowledgments

THE author acknowledges his indebtedness to the following persons and groups:

To his father and mother, who first aroused his interest in the life and career of Colonel Aaron Burr

To the members and friends of The Aaron Burr Association, who have helped to maintain and to stimulate that interest

To certain colleagues and associates who have impressed upon him the need for a retelling of the story of Colonel Aaron Burr

To his wife, who has made it possible for him to devote certain portions of his time to historical research and to writing, and who has assisted in the research, arrangement of materials and typing

Contents

AARON BURR, A.B., LL.D. (PRINCETON)

❊   ❊   ❊   ❊   ❊   ❊

Lt. Colonel in the Army of the American Revolution
Member of the Legislature, State of New York
Attorney General, State of New York
Land Commissioner, State of New York
United States Senator from the State of New York
Director, The Bank of the Manhattan Company
Chairman, Constitutional Convention,
State of New York
Vice President of the United States of America
Author of *The Journal of Aaron Burr*, Etc.

❊   ❊   ❊   ❊   ❊   ❊

Soldier, Lawyer, Banker, Educator, Statesman
World Traveler and Patron of the Arts
Devoted Husband, Father, and Grandfather

❊   ❊   ❊   ❊   ❊   ❊

Born Newark, New Jersey, February 6, 1756
Died Port Richmond, New York, September 14, 1836
Buried at Princeton, New Jersey, September 16, 1836

Introductory Note

MORE THAN two centuries have passed since the birth
of Aaron Burr. In some regards, time and events have
treated him in unkindly ways. During much of his life,
he worked against peculiar combinations of adverse circumstances. Since his death, one writer after another
has misinterpreted and misjudged him. In spite of such
treatment, in which the hand of fate and the pens of
his enemies seem to have combined their forces against
him, there have been some few Americans in each
period of history who have had a sincere appreciation
for his superior qualities, for his forceful personality, for
his positive leadership, and for his valuable services to
his fellow men and to his country. He has indeed been
the American Phoenix, rising again from one defeat
after another and surviving attacks which were meant
to erase his name from the pages of history or to mis-
represent him if his name persisted. The present study
represents an interpretation of his life which it is hoped
will help to place him in a favored and honored position
in the thoughts of his countrymen of the present generation.

CHAPTER I

The Parentage and Infancy
of Aaron Burr

IT WAS IN June, 1752, that the Rev. Aaron Burr* married Esther, one of the daughters of the Rev. Jonathan Edwards. At the time of his marriage, the Rev. Mr. Burr had attained the age of thirty-seven years. He also had established himself as a very successful man in two related fields: for some fifteen years, he had served as the pastor of the First Presbyterian Church of Newark, New Jersey; and more recently, he had succeeded the Rev. Jonathan Dickinson as President of the College of New Jersey (which later was to be known as Princeton University).†

---

* On page 1 of his book *Aaron Burr: A Biography* (Stokes, 1937), Nathan Schachner states that the immigrant ancestor of the Aaron Burr family in America was of German origin. His justification for this statement appears to be a reference to material in *The Private Journal*, to the effect that Aaron Burr found that he had "cousins" living in Germany when he was there in 1810 (Letter to Mr. J. G. Burr, in the Davis Edition, Vol. II, page 28). Genealogical research by members of the family in the present century indicates that their four immigrant ancestors named Burr came from England. It is assumed that these four men were brothers, or cousins, or that they were otherwise related to one another. As a consequence, their descendants consider themselves to be members of the same family group.

† The Rev. Jonathan Dickinson served as President of the college for less than a year, under the original charter, before his death. The Rev. Aaron Burr was the first President of the college under the new charter, which in many respects still serves as the basic document for Princeton University.

His bride was considerably younger; she was only twenty-one years of age. Her father ranked as the leading Calvinist theologian and philosopher of his era. He had given much of his time and personal attention to the education of his children, and Esther was quite adequately prepared to fill the social and educational position which she assumed as a result of her marriage.

The first child of the Rev. Aaron and Esther Burr was a daughter, born May 3, 1754. This little girl was named Sarah, after her grandmother, Sarah Edwards, but the nickname Sally was applied to her when she was a child and she continued to be known as Sally Burr during the entire span of her life. The second child born to the Burrs was a son, who was given his father's name, Aaron. The date of his birth was February 6, 1756.

Soon after the birth of Aaron Burr the Younger, the College of New Jersey was moved to its new location at Princeton, New Jersey, where the President had personally planned and directed the erection of Nassau Hall, which was then the largest single building in the English colonies. When the college moved to its new location, President Burr resigned his Newark pastorate and began to devote all his time and energy toward developing a great institution of learning. This called for considerable versatility, but he proved equal to the challenge. Already, he had written a Latin grammar that was in use not only in his own college but in other schools as well. In the matter of personnel, he recruited promising students for the college, and he chose the tutors who were associated with him in the teaching work. As a professor, he taught some classes himself, and of course, he was in full charge of matters affecting the behavior of the students. He supervised the keeping of the college records, and he was constantly concerned with the raising of funds—a task of no mean proportions.

His varied endeavors suddenly ended in a most tragic manner, however, for the Rev. Aaron Burr died on September 24, 1757, at the age of only forty-one years, as the result of overwork, exposure, and exhaustion. The trustees of the college chose his father-in-law, the Rev. Jonathan Edwards, to succeed him in the presidency.

President Edwards did not arrive at the village of Princeton until early in February, 1758. Upon his arrival, he found that the region surrounding the college was infested by an epidemic of smallpox. He was inoculated against the disease, and apparently as a result of this, he developed a fever. Six weeks later, on March 22, 1758, he died.

While her father was ill, Mrs. Esther Edwards Burr had contracted smallpox, and she died on April 7, 1758.

Both President Edwards and his daughter had been attended during their illness by Dr. William Shippen of Philadelphia, who now took the two Burr children to his own home in order to remove them from the area of smallpox infection. A few months later, their grandmother, Mrs. Sarah Pierrepont Edwards, made the long overland trip from her home in Stockbridge, Massachusetts to Philadelphia to get the children and take them back to Massachusetts with her. This trip proved to be too great a tax upon her physical endurance, and soon after her arrival in Pennsylvania, she also died.

Thus, before Aaron Burr the Younger reached the age of two years, he had lost his father, his mother, his grandfather, and his grandmother, all in quick succession.

By this series of natural events, those persons who ordinarily would have had the greatest influence in guiding the thoughts and acts of Aaron Burr were removed from the scene before they had had very long to serve in their normal capacities as parents and grandparents. Certainly the untimely death of the Rev. Aaron Burr and of Mrs. Esther Edwards Burr can be regarded as nothing short of calamitous for the two children. It was the first in a series of severe and adverse conditions which struck at Aaron Burr from time to time throughout his long life. In this particular case, he was too young to realize the implications of the death of his parents. Being an infant, he had to accept the decisions made for him by others, in this emergency.

ADDITIONAL REFERENCES

Burr, Aaron. *The Private Journal of Aaron Burr*, 2 vols. Ed. William H. Samson; publ. William K. Bixby. Rochester, N.Y.: The Genesee Press, 1903.

———. *Ibid.*, 2 vols. Ed. Matthew L. Davis. New York: Harper & Brothers, 1838.

Burr, Esther. *Esther Burr's Journal*, 2d ed. Ed. Jeremiah Eames Rankin. Washington, D.C.: Howard University Print, no date (probably about 1900).

Edwards, Jonathan. *Puritan Sage: Collected Writings of Jonathan Edwards.* Ed. Vergilius Ferm. New York: Library Publishers, 1953.

Miller, Perry. *Jonathan Edwards.* New York: William Sloane Associates, 1949. (The four chapters on "The External Biography.")

Schachner, Nathan. *Aaron Burr: A Biography.* New York: Frederick A. Stokes Company, 1937.

Todd, Charles Burr. *A General History of the Burr Family in America*, 4th ed. New York: The Knickerbocker Press, 1902.

CHAPTER II

Childhood and Youth

WHEN the hand of death removed their parents and grand-parents, the Burr orphans remained with the Shippen family for a short time, then became wards of their mother's brother, Timothy Edwards of Stockbridge, Massachusetts. Shortly before this, Timothy had married Rhoda Ogden, the sister of one of his tutors at the College of New Jersey.

In 1762 Timothy Edwards, his wife, and their Burr wards moved to Elizabethtown, New Jersey, where the Ogden family owned considerable real estate and where they operated a tannery well known throughout the colonies for the fine quality of its leathers. It was in Elizabethtown that the young Aaron Burr spent his childhood. His usual companion during this period was a boy of his own age, Matthias Ogden, who was the youngest brother of his Aunt Rhoda and who also was a member of the household of Timothy Edwards.

Timothy Edwards was a stern and unimaginative man who had good intentions but little or no knowledge of child psychology. Apparently he ruled the children with a heavy hand, but he also made provision for the proper education of his wards by employing a number of tutors. One of these tutors was Tapping Reeve, who fell in love with Sally Burr and later married her.

Uncle Timothy Edwards also proved to be a shrewd administrator of the Burr estate, so that the financial position of Aaron and his sister improved to a considerable extent during their minority. But as a foster father he failed to win the love or the confidence of the Burr children. Aaron reported later that whenever he committed any sort of misdemeanor, Uncle Timothy made him get down on his knees and ask God to forgive him. After the prayer was over, his uncle "beat him like a sack."

As a natural result of such treatment, Aaron tried to run away from home on several occasions. Once he got as far as the harbor and agreed to ship as a cabin boy on a schooner. Uncle Timothy managed to locate him before the ship sailed, and the disappointed youngster was forced to return with him to the Edwards household.

With the consent of his tutors, who believed that he was properly prepared, Aaron Burr applied for admission to the College of New Jersey when he was only eleven years old. It is possible that one of his reasons for this unseemly precipitousness about college entrance was his desire to escape from the immediate personal control of his uncle. The request was denied by Dr. John Witherspoon, who then was the President, so Aaron continued to study at the Edwards home in Elizabethtown under the direction of tutors until 1769, when he was admitted to the college as a member of the sophomore class. At Princeton, he studied the classics in their original Latin and Greek; he read widely in the fields of history, economics, and politics; he wrote a series of essays in English; he mastered the field of mathematics; and he made a number of firm friendships, and a few which proved to be not so firm when tried under tensions at a later date, with men who were to be associated with him throughout his long life.

Some of the notables among his college mates at Princeton were James Madison, James Monroe, William Patterson, Jonathan Dayton, Samuel Spring, Luther Martin, Philip Freneau, Lighthorse Harry Lee, Henry Brockholst Livingston, Morgan Lewis, Jonathan Mason, Hugh Breckenridge, and Matthias Ogden. There were others, too, but these names were destined to recur over and over again in incidents affecting the life of Aaron Burr.

He was graduated from the College of New Jersey in 1772 with an A.B. degree, Magna Cum Laude.

For a time, he considered the Presbyterian ministry as a life work, and he actually studied theology for some eight or nine months under Dr. Joseph Bellamy at Bethlehem, Connecticut. His readings led him to the unorthodox conclusion that "the way to Heaven is open to all alike," and he turned his attention to the law as his profession.

His study of law was done under the direction of his brother-in-law, Judge Tapping Reeve of Litchfield, Connecticut, who had married his sister Sally. It was while he was at Litchfield that Dorothy Quincy (John Hancock's fiancée), who was visiting there, described Aaron Burr as "a handsome young man with a pretty fortune."

As Aaron Burr began his study of law, he fully realized that there was a political ferment developing in the colonies. There were many people who were restive under the policies being pursued by King George III and his ministers. The spirit of revolution was abroad in the land, and in due time it led to open warfare.

In its effects upon the lives of individual men, war can develop quite a mixture of favorable and adverse elements. Such was the case in its various effects upon the life and career of Aaron Burr.

One immediate effect of the war had to do with his program of study. It interrupted his reading of law and his legal research. This interruption was to be four years in duration. From July, 1775, until July, 1779, his time, his energy, and his thinking were devoted entirely to the service of his country. He also spent most of his financial inheritance to assist the men who were in his military command.

ADDITIONAL REFERENCES

Knapp, Samuel S. *The Life of Aaron Burr.* New York: Wiley and Long, 1835.

Norris, Edwin M. *The Story of Princeton.* Boston: Little, Brown and Co., 1917.

Wandell, Samuel H., and Meade Minnigerode. *Aaron Burr,* 2 vols. New York: G. P. Putnam's Sons, 1925.

CHAPTER III

Service in the Army
of the Revolution

WHEN the news of battle came from Lexington and Concord, Aaron Burr abandoned the study of law at once. With his cousin, Matthias Ogden, he went to Cambridge and joined the Army of the Revolution. He was appointed captain (at the age of nineteen years) by General Washington, and soon afterward he set out on the difficult and hazardous trip through the northern wilderness as a member of General Arnold's ill-fated expedition to Canada. As an aide to General Montgomery, at Quebec, he gained well-deserved fame and a reputation for great daring and personal bravery. In the assault of the Americans upon the fortress of Quebec, Captain Burr was in the advance party, and it was he who prevented the British from gaining possession of his fallen leader's body. He returned to New York City as the bearer of secret dispatches telling of the unfavorable situation of the American forces that had been sent to Canada.

After a few weeks at the army headquarters in New York City, Washington sent him to General Israel Putnam, where he again served as an aide. This was the position that he held when the retreat from Long Island was ordered. In the process of this retreat, Aaron Burr, then holding the rank of major, saved an entire regiment from capture or destruction by the advancing British forces. In order to effect this exploit, he disregarded orders from officers who outranked him and consequently received no official commendation for it. The regiment was saved, however, and the men in it realized that this had been accomplished by the aggressiveness and leadership of a mere stripling named Major Burr.

After the retreat from Long Island, Aaron Burr participated in the Battle of White Plains. He was with Washington's forces at the Battle of Germantown in October, 1777, and he was given command of a strategic outpost during the terrible winter of 1777–78, when the Revolutionary Army was at Valley Forge.

He attained the rank of lieutenant colonel at the age of twenty-one and was assigned to the regiment of Colonel William Malcolm, then encamped at Ramapo, New Jersey. Colonel Malcolm had had no military training and promptly gave entire responsibility for the regiment to his competent and able Lieutenant Colonel.

At the Battle of Monmouth, Lieutenant Colonel Aaron Burr was put in charge of a brigade in Lord Stirling's command. Again he displayed great personal bravery and had his mount shot from under him, although he was not injured. During the engagement, he was dissatisfied with orders for the disposition of his men and did not hesitate to express his annoyance, so again his exploits did not receive official commendation.

Colonel Burr's final military assignment, before ill health caused him to resign from the army, was to the command of the highly important Westchester Lines, north of New York City. It was a difficult assignment, but he accomplished his mission with brilliant success. While serving here, he found that neither army supplies nor funds were being received, and he spent practically his entire personal fortune in feeding, clothing, and paying his troops. He took this action without having orders or directives for it, and the federal government never made any restitution to him for the sums he expended in this way.

The condition of his health had become so unfavorable that he felt compelled to submit his resignation from the army in March, 1779. Washington wrote him an appreciative letter, accepting the resignation, in April of that year.

Even after he had reverted to a civilian status, however,

Colonel Aaron Burr had further army experience. In June, he undertook and accomplished a difficult mission having to do with military intelligence for General Alexander McDougall.

Early in July, 1779, when he was in New Haven, Connecticut, Colonel Burr's illness had reached the point where it was necessary for him to remain in bed most of the time. On July 5, a strong force of British regulars, commanded by Generals Tryon and Garth, attacked the city. In spite of his weakened condition, Colonel Burr got up from his sickbed, rallied the local militia, and organized the students of Yale College in order to provide a partial defense for the city. This action greatly delayed the British advance and made possible the escape of many women and children.

After this final military exploit, he wholeheartedly gave his attention to regaining his health. He must also have been somewhat concerned about establishing the means for making a living, because he left the army without the financial assets that had been inherited from his father and augmented by his uncle.

ADDITIONAL REFERENCES

Livingston, William Farrand. *Israel Putnam.* New York: C. P. Putnam's Sons, 1901.

Parton, James. *Life and Times of Aaron Burr.* New York: Mason Brothers, 1857.

CHAPTER IV

First Marriage

On July 2, 1782, Colonel Aaron Burr and Mrs. Theodosia Bartow Prevost were married by the Rev. Benjamin Van der Linde, pastor of the Dutch Reformed Church at Paramus, New Jersey. Mrs. Prevost was the widow of a British army officer, Lieutenant Colonel Jacques Marcus Prevost, who had died in 1779 while on a military mission in the West Indies. She was also related by blood and by marriage to other officers serving under the British crown, but her loyalty to the cause of the American patriots was well known.

Colonel Burr's wife was several years older than he, and she was the mother of four children: Anne Louisa Prevost, Mary Louisa Prevost, Augustine James Frederick Prevost, and John Bartow Prevost. By his marriage Colonel Burr automatically became the stepfather of these four young people. The two boys became members of the Burr household, and in all respects Colonel Burr treated them as if they were his own sons. The two girls were reared by members of the Prevost family.

Mrs. Burr's father had been Theodosius Bartow, a well-to-do merchant of New York City. A number of her ancestors had been well-known people in the history of the British colonies, among them being Lieutenant Nicholas Stillwell of Virginia and later of New York City, and the Rev. John Bartow, the clergyman who established the first Episcopal parish in Westchester County, New York. After the death of her first husband, Theodosia's mother had remarried and she now was Mrs. deVisme.

The married life of Aaron and Theodosia Burr was a most

happy experience for both of them. They were very much in love with one another, and each of them possessed qualities of character upon which the other came to depend. They became the parents of four children, two boys and two girls, only one of whom lived to adulthood—the younger Theodosia, whom Colonel Burr idolized. The other three children died in their early infancy.

Aaron Burr supervised every step in his daughter's training and development, and he made of her one of the best-educated and most-accomplished women of her age. Nature had endowed the younger Theodosia with unusual beauty and grace as well as with a keen intellect. She responded readily to the regimen that her father established for her and pleased her tutors by the speed with which she mastered the equivalent of a college education.* She also was fond of the out-of-doors and excelled at skating and horseback riding.

About the year 1790, Mrs. Burr became ill and she remained a semi-invalid for four years until her death on May 18, 1794. The loss of his wife was another calamity and a very severe shock to the Colonel. It brought to a close a fine type of family relationship, and it removed from the Colonel's life an influence which had helped to give balance and direction to his brilliant progress in the world of which he was such an active and aggressive part.

Colonel Burr's reaction to the death of the elder Theodosia was not to seek a new wife. He looked to the younger Theodosia to serve as the hostess in their Richmond Hill mansion. Even though she was only eleven years old when her mother died, this young lady proved to be quite able to fulfill the social obligations that fell upon her. She presided over the mansion with dignity, grace, and charm during a period when many prominent Americans and foreign notables were her father's guests.†

---

* Theodosia's academic studies included Greek, Latin, French, German, moral philosophy, economic theory, classic and modern literature, ancient and modern history, and mathematics. She also studied music.

† Practically all of the politically and socially great Americans of this era, as well as many distinguished visitors from abroad, were guests at

In order to provide Theodosia a suitable companion of her own age, Colonel Burr took into his family circle Mlle Natalie de Lage de Volade. She was the daughter of Admiral de Lage de Volade of the French navy. Because of circumstances growing out of the French revolution, this young lady had been separated from her family and was stranded in New York City with only a nursemaid to care for her. In the Burr household, she received practically the same regard and attention that Theodosia received, and the two girls considered each other as adopted sisters. She never returned to France. When Theodosia married a South Carolinian, Natalie did also, her husband being the son of General Thomas Sumter.

When they were not together, Colonel Burr and Theodosia the Younger wrote frequent letters to each other—letters expressing such mutual love, confidence, and respect that they have been recognized as classics in this mode of expression.

On the evening before his duel with General Hamilton (the evening of July 10, 1804), her father wrote a letter for Theodosia. It contained the following famous paragraph:

> I am indebted to you, my dearest Theodosia, for a very great portion of the happiness which I have enjoyed in this life. You have completely satisfied all that my heart and affections had hoped or even wished.

And it was Theodosia who helped to encourage and sustain her father when he was experiencing severe tribulations, by a letter, dated August 1, 1809, which read, in part:

> I witness your extraordinary fortitude with new wonder at every new misfortune . . . you appear to

---

the Burr mansion at Richmond Hill, at one time or another. Among them were John Adams, John Jay, Alexander Hamilton, Rufus King, Marinus Willett, Thomas Jefferson, James Madison, James Monroe, the Clintons, the Livingstons, the Swartwouts, the Morrises, the Biddles, the Edwards, Joseph Brant (Chief Thayendanegea), Jerome Bonaparte, Prince Louis Philippe, Comte de Volney, Talleyrand, Sir John Temple, and many others.

me so superior, so elevated above all other men, I
contemplate you with such a strange mixture of
humility, admiration, reverence, love, and pride,
that very little superstition would be necessary to
make me worship you as a superior being . . . My
vanity would be greater if I had not been placed
so near you; and yet, my pride is our relationship.
I had rather not live than not be the daughter of
such a man.

ADDITIONAL REFERENCES

Groves, Joseph A. *Alstons and Allstons of North and South Carolina.*
Selma, Ala.: copyright by author, 1902.

Harden, John. *The Devil's Tramping Ground and Other North Carolina
Mystery Stories.* Chapel Hill: University of North Carolina Press, 1949.
(Chapter on "The Disappearance of Theodosia Burr.")

Smith, Dorothy Valentine. "Mrs. Prevost Requests the Honor of His Company . . ." *Manuscripts,* Vol. XI, No. 4 (Fall, 1959).

Stillwell, John E. *History of the Burr Portraits.* New York: privately
printed, 1928.

Van Doren, Mark, ed. *Correspondence of Aaron Burr and His Daughter,
Theodosia.* New York: Covici-Friede, Inc., 1929.

CHAPTER V

The Lawyer and Politician

AFTER he had regained a degree of good health following his service in the Army of the Revolution, Colonel Aaron Burr had resumed his interrupted study of law. During long hours he read from legal volumes and discussed the contents of the books with those who were guiding his work.

In the State of New York there was a regulation requiring law students to study for a period of several years before taking their examinations. Before this amount of time had passed, Colonel Burr was ready to be examined and the time limit was reduced in his case. He was licensed as an attorney on January 19, 1782, and on April 17 of that year, he was admitted to the bar.

His first law office was opened in Albany, where he quickly established himself and developed an extensive practice. He soon gained a reputation as a lawyer who was a master of courtroom procedure and an expert in the preparation of briefs. He almost never lost a case.

Toward the end of 1783, he moved to New York City, where his initial success in Albany was repeated on a larger scale.

The practice of law led naturally to the political arena, where the Colonel took the side of the Anti-Federalists and where he championed the cause of the common man.

The position that he took in the area of politics indicated original thinking and required considerable courage on his part. Because of his ancestry and the social position of his relatives, Colonel Burr had every right to consider himself a member of the elite, just as the leaders of the Federalists did. He chose the democratic point of view, however, giving practical support to his decision by a number of definite statements and concrete acts.

By establishing that group ownership of real estate qualified all members of the group as voters, he broke the political power of the few and the wealthy at a time when ownership of property was a prerequisite for the franchise in New York City and New York State.

By sponsoring a carefully worded enabling act in the state legislature, he made possible the establishment of the Manhattan Company, which, through its bank, broke the financial control of the Federalist monopoly in the banking field.*

By reorganizing the Society of St. Tammany (The Columbian Order) as a useful and helpful organization already established, he created the first American political machine.

By publicly espousing the cause of the French Revolution, he indicated clearly that his sympathies were with the masses of the people rather than with the self-appointed few who thought of themselves as aristocrats.

In each one of these developments and in others related to them, he incurred the bitter enmity of those entrenched in positions of power and of authority. It was a type of enmity that persisted over the years. Some whom he had defeated in the courts, at the polls, in the banking field, and on the floor of the legislature never missed any opportunity to strike back at him throughout the remainder of his life.

As a political leader, Colonel Burr helped to form the new party of Democratic-Republicans, which replaced the less well-defined group of Anti-Federalists. The place he came to occupy in the new party made him at least the equal of the Clintons and the Livingstons, in terms of political power, much to their surprise and chagrin. The jealousies within the Republican group were almost as serious as was the opposition to them from the tradition-loving Federalists.

---

* The primary purpose of The Manhattan Company was to supply pure water for the city of New York, and this it did, for a considerable period of years.

During several terms, he was a member of the New York State Assembly. While serving in this capacity, Colonel Burr led the fight to abolish Negro slavery and he advocated the extension of greater educational facilities and political rights to women.

The Governor, George Clinton, appointed him to serve as Attorney General and Commissioner of Public Lands for the state. He accepted the appointment and proved to be a great success in these positions. Some of the decisions that he was called upon to make were of a basic nature, and certain of his official opinions still serve as precedents that are followed even today. Then the Governor offered him an appointment as a judge on the Supreme Court of the state, but he declined this because it would have removed him from the field of active politics. It is quite likely that the offer was actually made so that leadership of the new political party might be left to the Clintons and the Livingstons.

In 1791, Colonel Burr was chosen by the legislature of the State of New York to serve as one of the two United States Senators from that state. Many had assumed that the choice would be General Philip Schuyler, father-in-law of Alexander Hamilton. Burr accepted the election and served with distinction for six years as a member of the upper house of the Congress of the United States.

Although General Schuyler did become a United States Senator from New York at a later date, the members of the Schuyler-Hamilton clan never forgot that Burr had defeated them in the contest of 1791. Their bitter political enmity for the Colonel was apparent from time to time, on both the state and the national scenes.

In 1792, Colonel Burr received one electoral vote for the Presidency. It was cast by an elector from South Carolina as a tribute to the growing reputation of this young and vigorous political leader from New York City. In 1793 the Democratic-Republican members of the United States Congress recommended to the President that Burr be appointed Minister to France, but Washington was influenced by Hamilton to nominate James Monroe for that diplomatic post. During the X Y Z affair in 1797, John Adams indicated that he would like to appoint Colonel Burr to serve as brigadier general, but Hamilton (then second in command of the United States Army) opposed this recognition of his rival's claim to military advancement.

On a nationwide basis, the leader of the Democratic-Republicans was Thomas Jefferson of Virginia. Because of unforeseen consequences of the provisions for voting in the Electoral College, Jefferson had become Vice President under John Adams, the Federalist. As Vice President he had practically no power in the federal government, but he was in a strategic spot to maintain and to enhance his position as the undisputed leader of the new party.* It was Jefferson, in his role as a party leader, who recognized Aaron Burr's importance to the Democratic-Republican party in New York, New Jersey, and Connecticut. It was Jefferson who designated Burr as the vice-presidential candidate in 1796 and again in 1800. And he definitely chose Burr when either a Clinton or a Livingston was available as a running mate.

Having chosen Burr as his running mate for the election of 1796, Jefferson indulged in a highly questionable political procedure. He refrained from asking the electors to cast their votes for the party team of Jefferson and Burr. As a consequence, Jefferson received 68 electoral votes in 1796 while Burr received only 30. The other Democratic-Republican electoral votes were widely scattered among "favorite sons" who had no possible

---

* The French Revolution had an amazing impact upon some segments of the American public, especially in New York and some other cities. The fall of King Louis XVI and his government was hailed as a great stride forward for universal democracy. A number of Jacobin Clubs sprang into being. Some men began to address one another as "Citizen." Liberty poles were erected at some street corners and in public squares. Liberty caps were prominently displayed. By all of this, the new party of Democratic-Republicans benefited and the Federalists lost ground. There began to be some disillusionment concerning the national leaders of the Federalist party. The Jay Treaty with Great Britain was denounced in flaming oratory at various public meetings, and Hamilton was even pelted with eggs and stones when he sought to defend it.

chance to win any elective position in the federal government. One of the chief offenders in this process was the Commonwealth of Virginia, in which only one elector voted for Burr although all of them voted for Jefferson!

Naturally, Burr wanted assurances that this condition would not be repeated in the election of 1800. If the new party was to win, he wanted both of its candidates to assume office—one as President and the other as Vice President. Apparently he received assurances of party regularity in the Electoral College.

Everyone who studied the political situation seemed to realize that the result of the national election of 1800 hinged upon what might happen in New York. John Jay had carried the state for the Federalists in the contest for the governorship in 1799. It was Aaron Burr's task to reverse this situation and to carry it for the Democratic-Republicans in 1800.

By a series of brilliant political maneuvers, the seemingly impossible was accomplished. Burr assembled a relatively small group of political lieutenants (dubbed by Theodosia "the Tenth Legion"). This little group met regularly with their leader, usually at Martling's Tavern, and he depended upon their help in carrying his political strategy into successful action.*

The list of eligible voters was expanded by means of the joint ownership of various parcels of real estate. Colonel Burr helped various small groups of individuals to purchase, as joint owners, certain vacant lots within the city limits. As joint tenants, each member of such groups had the right to register as a voter. The Colonel and his associates chose the members of these groups very carefully. They selected relatively obscure men who were known to have expressed some interest in political affairs. All of them could be depended upon to cast their votes in favor of the Democratic-Republican candidates for office, rather than for the Federalists.

Announcement of Democratic-Republican candidates for the state legislature was delayed until as late as was possible. Then,

---

* See Appendix B, "The Martlings."

after the Federalists had posted a list of relatively unknown men, Burr published the names of the candidates of the new party. The list included George Clinton, Horatio Gates, Brockholst Livingston, Samuel Osgood, John Swartwout, Henry Rutgers, Elias Nexen, Thomas Storm, George Warner, Philip I. Arcularius, James Hunt, and Ezekiel Robbins. Every one of them was well known to the people of New York in that generation. And Burr himself was nominated for the State Assembly by his friends in Orange County.

The Burr lieutenants now prepared card indexes of registered voters and of those who could be asked to contribute to the party fund. Systematic plans were made for calling upon all who were listed.

And the Society of St. Tammany (or Columbian Order) was expanded and revamped into an effective political machine.

At the last minute, both parties flooded New York City with handbills. Hamilton and his immediate friends rode around the city, mounted on horses, haranguing little groups of voters wherever they could be assembled. But Burr's astute planning succeeded. The State of New York elected a Democratic- Republican legislature, and that meant a shift of twelve electoral votes to the new political party.

It was well for the Republicans that Burr had succeeded in his difficult assignment because President John Adams actually received more electoral votes (aside from the 12 from New York) in the election of 1800 than he had received in the election of 1796. It was the new alignment of the votes of the state of New York which turned the political tide.*

When the electoral vote was counted in January, 1801 (with Jefferson presiding over the tabulation because of his position as Vice President), the result was Jefferson 73, Burr 73, Adams 65, Pinckney 64, Jay 1. The victory of the new party became an accomplished fact—a fact made possible only through the surprising success of Aaron Burr and his loyal followers in a state that previously had been in the Federalist column.

---

* See Appendix A for tabulation of electoral votes in the national elections of 1792, 1796, and 1800.

But now there were two Presidents-elect. Jefferson and Burr stood tied for the first position with 73 votes each. Every Republican elector had respected the demand for full support of the party ticket.

By the provisions of the Constitution, the tie had to be resolved by the House of Representatives—not the newly elected House but the holdover, or "lame duck," House in which the Federalists held a majority of the votes.

If Colonel Burr had been ruled by personal ambition, or if he had been an opportunist, he could have deserted his party at this point. There can be absolutely no doubt that the Federalists in the House were ready, willing, and able to make a deal with him and to elect him to the Presidency, if he would have made even a token move in their direction. This he definitely refused to do.

No one knows just what Mr. Jefferson expected Colonel Burr to do after the tie vote in the Electoral College was made known. Some modern commentators have suggested that the Colonel should have traveled to Washington and that he should have done two things upon his arrival there: (1) issued a public statement urging the election of Mr. Jefferson to the Presidency, and (2) interviewed the Federalist members of the House of Representatives urging them to cast their votes for Jefferson. It is quite evident that Colonel Burr did not consider such extreme measures to be necessary. He remained in Albany and he wrote a letter expressing his desires. This letter, dated December 16, 1800, was addressed to Congressman Samuel Smith of Maryland, and in it he clearly stated that he considered Mr. Jefferson to be the proper person to receive the Presidency. General Smith was to make this point of view known to other members of the Congress. And on December 23, Colonel Burr wrote to Mr. Jefferson, expressing surprise that Rhode Island had not cast one of its second-place votes for another person in order to prevent a tie. This letter also indicated that Colonel Burr expected Mr. Jefferson to receive the votes of at least nine states for the presidency when the voting started in the House of Representatives.

The House assembled in Washington, D.C., for its momentous decision in February, 1801. Colonel Burr was still in Albany, attending to his duties as a member of the New York State Assembly and arranging the details of Theodosia's wedding to Colonel Joseph Alston of South Carolina. He made no move to influence the vote other than by his letter to General Smith. Jefferson was present in Washington during the voting in the House and was in constant consultation with certain advisers and supporters who were working to secure the Presidency for him.

In spite of Burr's desires—and in spite of Hamilton's frenzied opposition—most of the Federalists in the House voted for Burr and the result was another tie.

After a week of indecisive votes and a great deal of political excitement, Jefferson finally was elected President on the thirty-sixth ballot (February 17, 1801), and Burr became the prospective Vice President, as he had anticipated.

This decision, that Mr. Jefferson should become President and that Colonel Burr should become Vice President, was the greatest determining element in the subsequent lives of both of these men and in their relationship with each other from that day forward. This decision not only gave Mr. Jefferson the first position; it made it possible for him to choose his successor and to exercise control over the Presidency for twenty-four years. This decision not only gave Colonel Burr the second position; it made it impossible for him to control his own political future.

Of course there were a number of imponderables in the picture, the chief one being that Mr. Jefferson might not live to complete his presidential term of four years. If he had died before the election of 1804, while serving as the Chief Executive, then all would have changed. Colonel Burr would have succeeded to the presidency and the center of gravity for the Republican party would have shifted away from Virginia to the state of New York.*

There were also other uncertainties. Colonel Burr might have

---

* Jefferson was born on April 13, 1743, and Burr was born on February 6, 1756. Consequently, Jefferson was almost thirteen years older than Burr.

accepted the decision as marking the end of his own political ambitions. He might have became a "yes man" for Mr. Jefferson and might have consulted him, and he might have followed his advice on every political detail presented to the new administration. To have acted in such a manner would have required an entire remolding of the Colonel's personality, however.

Some of the imponderables were quite beyond the control of either Jefferson or Burr. Who would have predicted in February, 1801, the meteoric rise of Napoleon to become Emperor of France and virtual dictator of half of Europe? Who would have predicted, when Jefferson took office, that the United States would purchase any part of Louisiana, let alone the entire territory? Who would have predicted the spirit of unrest that developed among the American settlers in the region beyond the Appalachians? Yet these unexpected factors were destined to play dominant roles in the lives of both the new President and the new Vice President.

The chances are that only Mr. Jefferson fully realized how important the decision about the presidency really was. Only he knew that Colonel Burr had been used as the means of securing the essential electoral votes of the State of New York and that he now was to be avoided, carefully excluded from all patronage, and ultimately to be replaced as Vice President by George Clinton, whose faction of the Democratic-Republican party now was to be built up in New York, but who was too old to pose any threat to the line of succession in the Virginia dynasty of Presidents.

Colonel Burr, still in Albany, fully expected that his political lieutenants and followers would receive suitable federal appointments in the new administration and that he would succeed Jefferson to the first position as Jefferson had succeeded Adams and as Adams had succeeded Washington. He was young and could afford to serve in the vice-presidency for four years—even for eight years, if necessary.

Gradually, the true political situation became apparent. Mr. Jefferson did not ask Colonel Burr for any suggestions about the proper men to fill federal positions. It developed that Mr. Jef-

ferson now looked upon Colonel Burr as an enemy—as a political power, once having been used to attain a goal, which now
was to be crushed and removed in order to attain a greater
goal. The President became committed to the establishment of
a whole line of Virginians who would serve as Presidents: himself, Madison, Monroe, and perhaps others. The one great threat
to such a line of succession was Vice President Aaron Burr. It
became clear to Jefferson that Burr's political prestige must be
destroyed at once and by no halfway measures. In order to
accomplish Jefferson's political plans, Burr had to be crushed.

The first step was to deny political rewards to all of Burr's
lieutenants. Not one of the Vice President's supporters received
any recognition after the new administration went into office
on March 4, 1801. Many appointments were made in the state
of New York, but all of them went to the Clinton and the
Livingston factions of the Republican party.* Jefferson knew
that any politician who wins an election is expected to reward
his followers, but he made it impossible for Burr to give proper
recognition to those who had worked so hard and so successfully in New York to win the election of 1800 for the Democratic-Republican party. The Burr political machine was thrown
into complete confusion and started to disintegrate. Only a few
personal friends continued to constitute "The Tenth Legion."

In spite of the political neglect with which the new President dealt with Colonel Burr, the Vice President refused to be
relegated to a place of political obscurity.

During the four years of Colonel Burr's service as Vice President of the United States (March, 1801–March, 1805), the
Louisiana Purchase was negotiated and approved; Ohio became
the seventeenth state in the Federal Union; the Twelfth Amendment was added to the United States Constitution; the naval
war with Tripoli was fought; the status of the federal judiciary
was determined; the Lewis and Clark Expedition was authorized
and that overland exploration party actually started its trek into

---

* The Livingstons received only token recognition. Most of the political
plums which were significant in developing party strength went to the
Clinton faction of the new party.

the great Northwest. In all these matters, Colonel Burr had as full a part as it was possible for a Vice President to have at that period in American history. As a matter of fact, he had a more active part in the making of decisions than most Vice Presidents have had because during one half of the four-year period the United States Senate was almost equally divided between the Federalists and the Democratic-Republicans. Consequently, Colonel Burr was able to cast the deciding vote in the Senate on a number of important issues.

He continued to maintain his residence in New York City, and he also had an apartment in Washington, D.C. His legal and political interests made necessary a considerable amount of travel to Albany, New York City, and Philadelphia. He also made trips to South Carolina, where Theodosia and her family were living.

In the midst of the turbulent political currents in which he was involved, he also found time to visit Princeton on many occasions. In 1802, his alma mater recognized his achievements by granting him its highest academic honor, the LL.D. degree.

When the time came for another national election, in 1804, Colonel Burr was not even mentioned as a possible candidate of his party, either for the Presidency or for the Vice Presidency. The choice went to Mr. Jefferson as the candidate for President and to George Clinton for Vice President. Clinton had served as Governor of New York for several terms. He was not a Virginian, of course, and neither was he young, vigorous, or ambitious. He fulfilled the traditional provision of being from another state, without presenting any challenge to the succession in the Virginia dynasty.

Colonel Burr's direct answer to the shabby treatment which he had received from those elements that controlled the Democratic-Republican party was to become a candidate for the governorship in New York in the spring of 1804. In this election, it was necessary for him to be listed as an Independent because by that time, the Democratic-Republican party in the state was under the complete control of Jefferson's appointees, their friends, and their relatives.

It was a crucial contest. If Colonel Burr could be elected to serve as Governor of the State of New York, his political star would be in its ascendency again. Victory also would mean that Jefferson would be challenged for control of the party on a national scale. Not only New York but also New England and perhaps New Jersey would line up in any political aspirations that Colonel Burr might have in the East. On the other hand, defeat for Burr would mean that the Virginians would continue in the Presidency, that the Clintons would control the State of New York, and that the Colonel's only chance for political preferment would have to come from the region beyond the mountains—the new West.

As might have been expected, the campaign proved to be an especially bitter one. The regular party workers within the Democratic-Republican and the Federalist ranks used tactics of a highly questionable nature. The printed folders and handbills which they distributed attacked Colonel Burr in every possible way. The most lurid and objectionable charges were made at the very last minute on the day preceeding the election, so that there was no opportunity to answer them and to show how false they were.

The result was a definite victory for the regular Democratic-Republican party organization and its candidate, Judge Morgan Lewis.

Even more serious for Colonel Burr than his defeat at the polls was the fact that the paid pamphleteers of his opponents had written scurrilous materials that had been distributed far and wide, not only in New York but in other eastern states also. These broadsides contained biased half-truths and outright lies reflecting adversely upon the deeds, motives, and character of Colonel Burr. Some of the falsehoods and innuendoes contained in this campaign literature have been repeated as facts down through the years. They have been largely responsible for much of the unwarranted abuse that has been heaped upon him since that time.

The immediate effects of the insulting comments, the campaign speeches, and libelous literature were more far-reaching than the election results themselves. Certain statements led to challenges. These were accepted and duels were fought. And the duels changed the normal course that history seemed to be taking for the principals who were involved. When the swords clashed and the pistols barked, they set up waves of opinion as well as of sound.

ADDITIONAL REFERENCES

Annals of Congress, The. Washington, D.C.: Gales and Seaton, 1791-97, 1801-5. (Alternate title: *The Debates and Proceedings in the Congress of the United States.*)

Brown, Everett Somerville, ed. *William Plumer's Memorandum of Proceedings in the United States Senate, 1803-1807.* New York: The Macmillan Co., 1923.

Burns, Edward McN., and Harris I. Effross. "The Democracy of Aaron Burr." *Proceedings of the New Jersey Historical Society,* April, 1954.

Morris, Richard B. "List of 300 Notable Americans." *The Saturday Review,* Vol. XXXVI, No. 47 (November 21, 1953), pages 68-71.

Steiner, Bernard C. *The Life and Correspondence of James McHenry.* Cleveland, Ohio: The Burrows Brothers Co., 1907.

CHAPTER VI

The Political Platform of Colonel Burr

THE political platform of Colonel Aaron Burr, in the national elections of 1796 and 1800, may be reconstructed to show his active support of the following "planks":

He supported the doctrine of the political equality of all men, regardless of birth, position, power, or wealth. He opposed the registration of voters on the basis of their ownership of real estate or personal property.

He opposed the institution of slavery, and he was instrumental in securing the abolition of slavery in the State of New York. He advocated emancipation in both the North and the South.

He believed in the complete separation of church and state but was not opposed to organized religion. He made frequent references to the power of prayer.

He favored the territorial expansion of the United States. He was among the first to see the desirability of adding the Floridas, Texas, and other western lands to the new nation.

He favored the rapid admission of new states to the American Union. He saw the prospect of a dozen new states in the area between the thirteen original ones and the Mississippi River.

He was strongly in favor of an independent system of courts, free from pressures from the executive and the legislative branches of the government, on both the state and the national levels.

He was a liberal in his position on banks and banking. By

the terms of his charter for The Manhattan Company, he broke the hold of the Federalists on the banking situation in New York City. He believed that the national economy would benefit if business and industry could borrow money more easily and at lower interest rates.

In foreign affairs, he favored a policy of friendship with both Great Britain and France. He also favored the creation of good relations with Scandinavia, Russia, and the German states. This policy did not extend to Spain; he considered warfare with Spain (over the Floridas and Texas) to be an inevitable consequence of the territorial needs of the new nation.

He favored independence from Spain for the Mexican nation and for the other Spanish colonies in America south of the Mexican territory.

He believed in more education for more people—including women. He evidenced his interest in this by generous gifts to various schools, colleges, and libraries.

He saw the need for new taxes but advocated only enough revenue to support the "necessary" expenses of government. He favored a balanced budget and careful budgetary controls.

He felt that the Constitution provided an adequate and appropriate balance between federal authority and states' rights.

He foresaw the collapse of the Federalist party and expected the party of Democratic-Republicans to replace it. His hope was for "the union of all honest men" in the new party.

He hoped for an era of international peace during which the United States could grow and develop from an economic standpoint. In order to maintain the peace, he considered that the United States should maintain an adequate army and navy.

And, of course, in the campaign of 1800, he favored the repeal of the alien and sedition laws which had been passed and approved during the Adams Administration.

ADDITIONAL REFERENCES

Jefferson, Thomas. *The Basic Writings of Thomas Jefferson*, reprint ed. Ed. Philip S. Foner. Garden City, N.Y.: Halcyon House, 1950.
Schachner, Nathan. *Aaron Burr: A Biography*. New York: Frederick A. Stokes Company, 1937.

CHAPTER VII

The Burr–Hamilton Duel

EVER SINCE their terms of service had begun in the Army of the Revolution, Aaron Burr and Alexander Hamilton had been rivals—as army officers, as bankers, as lawyers, and as political leaders. Yet on the surface at least, they posed as personal friends and they were entertained in each other's homes. Both of them were prominent members of the Society of the Cincinnati, of certain social and political clubs, and of many other organizations. The 1804 contest for the governorship of New York produced circumstances that finally broke this apparent friendship and led to the challenge to a duel. This encounter took place on July 11, 1804.

Both of the principals accepted the code duello as a naturaı and normal part of the mores of their age. Hamilton had challenged Commodore James Nicholson in 1795. His son, Philip Schuyler Hamilton, had been mortally wounded at Weehawken on November 23, 1801, by George I. Eacker, a New York lawyer and political figure. Colonel Burr had exchanged shots on the field of honor with John B. Church, Hamilton's brother-in-law, only about a week before the more famous encounter in 1804. There also were rumors that Colonel Burr and Samuel Broadhurst, a Hamilton lieutenant, had fought a duel, using swords as weapons, and that Broadhurst had received a flesh wound in that encounter.*

Early on the morning of July 11, two rowboats came across

---

* Many other men, prominent in the early history of the United States, had participated in duels and a number of deaths had resulted from them.

the Hudson River to a place called by the unusual name of Weehawken, in New Jersey. In the first boat were Colonel Burr and his friend, William P. Van Ness. In the second were General Alexander Hamilton, Judge Nathaniel Pendleton, and Dr. David Hosack. These men had agreed in advance to meet at this secluded spot and at this unusual hour. All of them came of their own free will, without being compelled or forced to keep this rendezvous.

Two of the men—Burr and Hamilton—came to shoot and to be shot at. Van Ness and Pendleton came to serve as seconds in the affair of honor. Dr. Hosack was prepared to attend either (or both) of the principals, as the need for medical service might arise.

After the most formal of greetings had been exchanged, the seconds proceeded with the arrangements for the duel. The distance of ten full paces was measured. Then they cast lots, first, for the choice of position and, second, to decide who should pronounce the commands: "Ready! Present! Fire!"

General Hamilton's second won the choice in both cases, and after he had made his decisions, the two antagonists took their allotted places. There was a slight delay while Hamilton adjusted his eyeglasses and glanced down the barrel of his pistol. He complained about the difficulty of sighting in the bright sunlight. When all was in order and Judge Pendleton had given the commands, two shots were fired. One pistol report came so close upon the other that it was impossible to tell which was first and which was second. The result was clear enough, however. After the two shots rang out and the two puffs of smoke rose in the morning air, Colonel Burr continued to stand erect while General Hamilton fell upon his side, his face contorted with pain.

Dr. Hosack rushed forward and examined the man who had fallen. The other principal was escorted away, his face shielded by an umbrella. All that the physician could do was to administer morphine to deaden the pain that General Hamilton was suffering. The boatmen were called, and they carried the wounded duelist down the steep slope to the river edge.

Again the two rowboats crossed the Hudson, this time toward Manhattan. Colonel Burr returned to his home at Richmond Hill, where he studied his law books and directed the work of his gardeners while awaiting developments. General Hamilton's physical condition had been made much worse by the long trip in an open boat. He was carried to the home of his friend, Mr. Bayard, and there he died on July 13. Whether his death was inevitable or whether it might have been prevented by proper medical and surgical treatment never has been authoritatively determined.* There can be no doubt, however, that the circumstances of his death helped to raise him to his status as one of America's national heroes.

Immediately after the duel, legends began to arise and to be associated with the facts in the case. For example, it was said that Hamilton had tried to avoid the duel and that Burr had forced it upon him. The correspondence between the two men has been preserved and published. A careful reading of it indicates that such was not the case. Burr asked for an explanation of certain remarks that Hamilton had made about him. Hamilton quibbled and procrastinated but did not explain. It was only after a number of letters had been exchanged that the challenge was issued and accepted.

Then it was reported that General Hamilton had decided to withhold his fire rather than to shoot at Colonel Burr. This legend goes even so far as to report that while he was lying in the boat after having been wounded, he cautioned Judge Pendleton to be careful in handling his pistol, because it still was loaded. Unfortunately, the force of this story is seriously impaired because only one-third of the General's admirers support it. Another third of them say that Hamilton's shot was the

---

* An amazing factor in the duel, and one that seldom has been recognized, is the fact that the pistols which General Hamilton brought to Weehawken Heights with him—the brace of pistols actually used in the duel—were not standard dueling pistols at all. They were of larger caliber than those specified in the dueling code of that day. If the weapons had been of the weight or bore specified in the recognized code, then Hamilton's wound would have been a less serious one.

first one fired and that he deliberately aimed well above Burr's head. Then another third admit that Hamilton fired his pistol, but their story is that he fired involuntarily because his hand contracted when he felt the piercing pain of his adversary's bullet in his side.

The two seconds, who were present at the duel and who were eyewitnesses to the event, differed in their reports as to just what happened. The New York City newspapers carried column after column of conflicting reports. Various details were presented and later were denied.

The newspaper stories were not the only tales that have been used to embroider the actual situation that did occur at Weehawken. It seems a great shame that so much fiction has entered into this scene; its true circumstances were packed with enough drama to make it a very remarkable incident in the history of America.

There was immediate popular reaction to the duel and its consequences, not only in New York and New Jersey but also in other parts of the country.

Before the duel, Hamilton had fallen to the status of a discredited politician. The Federalist party, in which he had been a powerful figure, was disintegrating. Leadership in the political field was passing into the hands of new people. But overnight, as a result of the duel, he became a martyr. His funeral was attended by a huge throng of people. His friends collected funds to pay his debts (more than $50,000). His widow was accorded a place of honor at various political functions as long as she lived.

For Aaron Burr there was bitter condemnation. The result of the duel was used for partisan political purposes in his case and the Vice President became the object of vicious attack. Inflammatory articles were published to discredit him and to bring him to a place of dishonor in the thoughts of the people.

In New York, he was charged with a misdemeanor. In New Jersey, he was indicted for murder.

In the face of such a combination of adverse elements, it was expedient for Colonel Burr to leave New York City. Accordingly, he made a trip to East Florida and spent some time in exploring that region. This expedition gave him the opportunity to study the Spanish colonial system at first hand, a fact that had a direct bearing upon some of his future behavior.

Then, after a brief visit with the Alstons in South Carolina, he went to Washington and resumed his duties as Vice President of the United States. Enough time had passed so that his reappearance in the national capital was taken as a matter of course.

ADDITIONAL REFERENCES

King, Charles R., ed. *The Life and Correspondence of Rufus King*, 6 vols. New York: G. P. Putnam's Sons, 1894-1900.

Schachner, Nathan. *Alexander Hamilton*. New York: D. Appleton-Century Co., Inc., 1946.

Seitz, Don C. *Famous American Duels*. New York: Thomas Y. Crowell Co., 1929.

Syrett, Harold C., and Jean G. Cooke, eds. *Interview in Weehawken*. Middletown, Conn.: Wesleyan University Press, 1960.

CHAPTER VIII

The Federal Judiciary

By THE election of 1800, the new party of Democratic-Republicans had gained control of the executive and the legislative branches of the federal government, but the federal judiciary continued to be staffed entirely by Federalists who had been appointed by Washington and Adams. A planned program now was launched in order to bring the courts into the new political fold.

The first step in this process was taken successfully when the National Judiciary Act of 1801 was repealed in March, 1802. The second step was to make the way clear for the replacement of Federalist judges by Republican appointees. Success in this step would require some adroit political maneuvering, for the judges had been appointed for life and could be removed only by the process of impeachment or by death. Jefferson decided that the traditional theory of impeachment might be redefined in order to accomplish the result he fervently desired.

In the eyes of the President, this matter of removing judges took on new importance and received additional impetus because of the tenor of certain decisions being handed down in important cases then before the federal courts. The most far-reaching of these was the celebrated case of Marbury *vs*. Madison, certainly a classic in its field. In their decisions on this and in other cases, Chief Justice John Marshall and his Associate Justices of the Supreme Court were expressing their belief in the independence of the courts. They were enunciating the theory that the Supreme Court of the United States could declare unconstitutional an act of Congress or an Executive Order. They were taking the position that the Supreme Court could send a writ of mandamus to a member of the President's Cabinet.

The Federalist John Marshall and his Federalist Associate Justices were establishing and maintaining the fact that the courts constituted an independent element in the American form of government, and that the judiciary branch was equal in rights and powers to the executive and the legislative branches.

This doctrine concerning an independent judiciary was, in reality, what now came under attack. Even before the repeal of the National Judiciary Act of 1801 the machinery had been set in motion to grind out the second phase of Jefferson's proposed program to accomplish this end.

The opening gun in the battle to remove the Federalist judges was fired against Judge Alexander Addison, of Pennsylvania. A petition demanding his impeachment and removal from office was presented to the Pennsylvania House of Representatives on January 11, 1802. Articles of impeachment were prepared and sent to the Pennsylvania State Senate on March 23, 1802. There, the Republican majority took speedy action and in spite of an able defense, the Judge was convicted and ordered removed on January 26, 1803. This case was considered as setting a precedent upon which others could be fought with assurance of success. Addison had defended himself by reference to classic examples in the law. He clearly stood upon the conservative point of view exalting an independent judiciary. He asserted that it was the exclusive province of the courts to pass upon the constitutionality of legislative acts. He argued that no judge could be impeached for any offense unless he also could be indicted for that same offense. But the Republicans put forth a new theory, namely, that a judge might be removed from the bench as a result of any behavior or any judicial opinion at variance with the prevailing desires of the dominant party of the legislature then in power.

Having won a case on one level, the President's party now moved to a higher level. Within ten days after Addison was removed, Jefferson suggested the impeachment of Judge John

Pickering of the United States Court for the District of New Hampshire. This suggestion was contained in a message to the House of Representatives dated February 4, 1803. The preparation of articles of impeachment was started at once, but quite a period of time elapsed before the trial was held. Part of the delay was caused by the fact that Judge Pickering had evidently become insane. Finally the trial was held, as the President desired. It ended on March 12, 1804, and the United States Senate found the obviously demented judge to be guilty of High Crimes and Misdemeanors. The vote was 19 to 7. Just what Vice President Burr thought of this procedure and of this verdict is not clear. No matter what his thoughts may have been, he certainly observed, with keen insight, the unfolding of Jefferson's well-laid plan to bring the judiciary within the control of the other two branches of government. The chances are that Colonel Burr, being a lawyer first and a politician afterward, did not approve of what the President was attempting to do, regardless of its relationship to party politics.

The removal of Addison and Pickering accounted for the spadework and general foundation of the more important aspects of the President's plan. Surely with these precedents established, Jefferson's next logical step was to move boldly upon his main objective: the Supreme Court of the United States.

There was not long to wait for such a development. Indeed, the public already had been prepared. Associate Justice Samuel Chase had been singled out as the next victim; a series of pamphlets had been prepared, attacking him; and these had been widely distributed and read. So far as the administration could do it, Chase was branded as a guilty man even before any move was made to impeach him.

After the verdict had been secured against Pickering, the matter rapidly was brought to a head. On the same day that the Senate convicted the New Hampshire judge, the House voted to impeach Samuel Chase! The ambitious and excitable Congressman John Randolph of Roanoke was appointed by the House to lead the prosecution of the aged and plain-spoken Federalist Justice.

The articles of impeachment drawn up by Randolph and his associates in the House were voluminous and all-inclusive. No unusual perception was needed to see that if the prosecution were successful, not only Chase but also Marshall and the other Federalists on the supreme bench with him would be removed.

The date for the trial to begin was set as January 2, 1805, giving both sides some time to prepare for the proceedings.

This was the stage where matters stood at the end of March, 1804, when the Vice President saw fit to absent himself from the national capital.

Aaron Burr left Washington and gave his personal attention to his unsuccessful political contest with Judge Morgan Lewis in the State of New York. Then there were other matters to claim his attention before his return to the national capital on November 5: the duels with Samuel Bradhurst and with General Hamilton; a serious courtship with "Celeste" in Philadelphia; a public reception at which he was the guest of honor in Savannah, Georgia; a sight-seeing trip to the Spanish colony of East Florida; and a brief visit with his daughter, Mrs. Theodosia Burr Alston, and her family in South Carolina.

When November 5 arrived, he was back in Washington again. On that day, he rose early, dressed with extreme care, had a light breakfast, and rode to the Capitol in his carriage. He entered the Senate chamber quietly and watched carefully to see how he might be received. He noticed that most of the Federalists were definitely reserved or cool. Some bowed but did not speak to him. There were a few who turned their backs as he passed. But the greatest change was on the part of the Republicans. There could be no doubt about it; they definitely reacted in a manner that was cordial—indeed, the Republicans were more than ever attentive to him. Accepting both the affected coolness of the Federalists and the fawning interest of the Republicans without any outward show of emotion, he mounted the rostrum and called the Senate to order.

It soon became apparent that the new marks of cordiality being shown Colonel Burr by his party members in the Senate were shared by many others in the Administration. Perhaps someone close to Jefferson had passed the word along that the official attitude toward the Vice President had changed. Jefferson now perceived that Aaron Burr held the key which would open or close the door of success in his current program of action dealing with the courts.

The Republican leaders had to revise their former attitude of isolating Aaron Burr. They were frank enough and practical enough to recognize that the success or failure of their designs upon the federal judiciary rested in his hands. As President of the Senate, he would preside at the court of impeachment for the case of Associate Justice Chase. His rulings on the admissibility of evidence would be final. His attitude would affect the votes of several Senators. His decisions on procedure might control the final result. In such a situation, there was only one course to follow: Aaron Burr must be treated with new deference and renewed respect. His immediate political desires must be ascertained and at least some effort must be made to satisfy them.

His invitations to White House dinners suddenly were more numerous. At least once each week, he was a guest at the President's table. Members of the Cabinet consulted him upon matters of state. He was seen riding with Mr. Madison, the Secretary of State. Senator Giles of Virginia personally secured the signatures of nearly all the Republican Senators to a petition on the Vice President's behalf to the Governor of New Jersey, where he had been indicted for murder.

The matter of the petition to Governor Bloomfield deserves special attention. It was no mere partisan document asking for a political favor, but a carefully prepared legal statement showing that personal prejudice was involved in the indictment of Colonel Burr. No indictment had been made affecting the two seconds: Mr. Van Ness and Mr. Pendleton. Yet in the eyes of the law, if the Vice President had been guilty of a crime, they were equally guilty. Nor had the constituted authorities in New Jersey brought indictments against other well-known duelists of that period. There had been no prosecution of Henry Brockholst

Livingson when he had killed the Federalist, James Jones, in a
duel at Weehawken. Nor had there been any legal action when
the young Philip Schuyler Hamilton had fallen, mortally
wounded, on November 23, 1801, in a duel with a Republican
lawyer of New York City named George I. Eacker. These and
other pertinent facts were pointed out to the Governor, for his
consideration.

In addition to other favors and marks of attention, the
President made some belated nominations calculated to please
the man who would preside over the Senate of the United States
during the attempt to make the judiciary subservient to the
executive and legislative branches of the government.

Colonel Burr's stepson, John Bartow Prevost, was named for
the post of Judge of the Superior Court at New Orleans. Dr.
Joseph Brown, husband of the deceased Mrs. Burr's half sister,
"Katy" deVisme, was proposed for Secretary of the Louisiana
Territory. General James Wilkinson, already the Commanding
General of the United States Army (and at this period assumed
to be a close personal friend of the Vice President) was nominated to serve—in addition to his military duties—as the Territorial Governor of Upper Louisiana. It may even have
happened that someone close to the President dropped vague
hints about a Cabinet post or an appointment in the diplomatic
service for the Vice President himself, after March 4, 1805.

Such tardy recognition of Aaron Burr's legitimate claims to
a share of party patronage by Jefferson must have been the
source of a certain amount of quiet sardonic amusement to the
Colonel. But these crude and rather transparent tactics had no
perceptible effect upon his attitude in the impeachment trial
about to begin.

When January 2, 1805, arrived, Justice Chase appeared before
the Senate of the United States and requested further delay in
the consideration of the charges which the House of Representatives had presented against him. He indicated that the preparation of his defense was not complete and asked that the matter
be deferred until the next session. The Senate granted him only
one additional month of delay and ordered him to reappear on

February 4. It was evident that the Republican senators expected the trial to be a brief one—it would have to end before March 4, 1805, when the session of Congress closed.

By formal vote of the Senate, all the detailed arrangements for conducting the momentous impeachment trial were left in the hands of the Vice President. All too clearly, he realized that this event might mark his final appearance as a holder of public office. Perhaps it was partly on this account that he decided to make the occasion a memorable one, so far as that was within his power. He accomplished this purpose, first, by the elaborate and colorful setting that he caused to be arranged and, second, by his own dress, bearing, deportment, and rulings during the progress of the trial.

Following his explicit directions, a crew of workmen transformed the plain and severe Senate chamber into an elaborate stage, where a great drama was about to be performed. It blazed with bright colors and reflected a type of splendor uncommon in the city of Washington in that era.

The rostrum of the presiding officer was left unchanged, and from this commanding spot the Vice President of the United States would control the dramatic proceedings. To the right and left of the rostrum extended two rows of desks, covered with crimson cloth. In all, there were thirty-four of these—one for each United States Senator. From the back wall, extending into the room, were three rows of benches, arranged in tiers. These were covered with green cloth and were reserved for the members of the House of Representatives. At the right end of the House benches was an enclosure or box, with upholstered seats. These were for the members of the Cabinet. The permanent gallery was left unchanged, and as usual, it was available to the general public. Beneath it, another temporary gallery had been built. The ends of this sub-gallery were rounded out to form boxes. This entire temporary structure was covered with green cloth, and the same cloth was draped over the balustrade. Special tickets of admission to the sub-gallery and boxes were issued to Senators, Congressmen, Cabinet members, Justices of the Supreme Court, Ministers of foreign countries, and others. These

tickets were used by the ladies of their families, who attended
in considerable numbers, dressed in the height of fashion. There
was an open passageway leading from the door to the rostrum
of the presiding officer. This passageway was flanked by enclo-
sures or boxes that were draped with blue cloth and the chairs
in them were covered with cloth of the same color. These
boxes were occupied by the managers from the House and by
the lawyers for the defense. There was a similar box for the
members of the Supreme Court and one for the accused Justice.
The flag of the United States provided a final spot of brilliant
color in the already colorful room.

The drama that was about to be worked out upon this stage
unfolded itself before a full house. On February 4, every seat
was occupied and all the important characters were there—save
one. Mr. Jefferson did not attend in person, but was kept advised
by messengers as to the progress of the affair. Here, for a month,
Aaron Burr was to be the leading character. After some slight
delay, he appeared at the door, and a temporary hush fell upon
the assemblage as he looked around the room. He seemed
taller than his five feet five inches. His slender, erect, well-
proportioned body exhibited all the poise and grace for which
he was famed. He had always dressed well for his role in the
Senate, but it was evident that his tailor had been especially
meticulous in making the new clothing that he had ordered for
this occasion. He seemed very much at ease, very sure of himself, as his dark hazel eyes took in every detail of the scene
before him. Slowly he walked down the aisle and stepped up to
his place in the center of this elaborate tableau. His behavior
was exactly correct in every way, leaving no chance for adverse
criticism from either side. He was entering into a difficult situation with an assurance and dignity that would reflect credit upon
him, upon the Senate, and upon the entire proceedings.

The Sergeant-at-Arms called the Senate to order as a Court
of Impeachment, and the trial began.

The rules for the procedure of the court (which the Senate
now had become) were explained in detail by Senator William

Branch Giles, who had been hand-picked as Jefferson's representative. In order to place him thus, Senator Abraham Venable had been induced to resign and Giles had been appointed by the Governor of Virginia to fill the vacancy thus artificially produced. There can be no doubt that the entire procedure was engineered at Jefferson's suggestion.

The leader of the attack by the majority party of the House of Representatives was the able but erratic John Randolph of Roanoke. At the time when he was chosen, it seemed that he had the personal courage, forensic ability, legal background, and party regularity to make him an ideal prosecutor. But during the month between January 2 and February 4, events had conspired to rob Randolph of some of his qualifications. The so-called Yazoo Fraud case had been before the House of Representatives during that month, and Randolph had broken with the Jefferson leadership concerning the financial settlement of the claims and concerning the political maneuvers adopted by the Administration in securing the approval of the settlement. By February 4, he no longer could qualify as a blind and willing follower of the President's dictates.

The other House managers, assisting Randolph in the prosecution, were Peter Early of Georgia, George W. Campbell of Tennessee, Joseph H. Nicholson of Maryland, and Caesar A. Rodney of Delaware.

An imposing array of legal talent represented the accused Justice. This group was made up of Luther Martin, Attorney General of Maryland; Joseph Hopkinson, author of "Hail, Columbia!" and a well-known lawyer; Philip Barton Key, the brother of Francis Scott Key; Charles Lee, who had been Attorney General of the United States under President Adams; and Robert Goodloe Harper, a former member of Congress and an eloquent orator.

As the trial began, there were a number of surprises, most of which grew out of the fact that Vice President Aaron Burr now took on the character of a presiding judge—a part which he played with supreme confidence and brilliant success.

Both sides were surprised by the fact that the trial really was a trial rather than an empty form. The Federalists had anticipated that the procedures would be only a legal farce. They could foresee no method of thwarting the President's designs upon the court. It certainly appeared that Jefferson held the situation securely within his control. On February 4, they assumed that Chase would be found guilty and that his removal from office would open the way for the removal of Marshall and the other Federalist Justices. The Republicans, likewise, had thought that the trial would be a mere matter of form. They anticipated that Jefferson's dictates would be binding upon the Vice President and upon the members of their party in the Senate and that Chase would be removed from the supreme bench by a strict party vote of 25 to 9, with only 23 Republican votes required for a conviction. They already knew the name of the member of their party who then would be nominated for Chase's position.

Most of the Senators had been surprised by Colonel Burr's elaborate stage setting for this trial, which they had thought about as a mere incident. When it was time for the proceedings to begin, they were further surprised to find the galleries crowded with eager spectators. Day after day, as the trial progressed, all of the space within the Senate chamber was filled to capacity and people who arrived late were turned away for lack of room.

As soon as the trial began, the Senators received still another surprise. The Vice President, behaving in a very punctilious manner himself, expected the same sort of behavior on the part of all who were involved. He exercised control over every detail, made the Senators sit in their appointed places, admonished them against eating cake and apples, forced them to give attention to the proceedings and to listen to the testimony of the witnesses.

Gradually it began to dawn upon all of them—and upon the man who sat in the White House, directing the prosecution and awaiting the result—that an honest, fair, and decent trial was being forced upon them by the Vice President. They began to comment to one another upon the fact that this was in reality a court of justice. Aaron Burr, acting as the presiding officer in it, was adding one more precedent establishing the fact that all American citizens, no matter how high or low their stations, were entitled to equal justice before the law. Here was to be no presumption of guilt unless guilt could be proven by due process of law. Jefferson's tactic of implying Justice Chase's guilt in advance and of building up popular disapproval before the trial was being discredited.

A total of fifty-two witnesses gave testimony at the trial. Among them were John Marshall, Chief Justice of the Supreme Court of the United States, and his brother, William Marshall, of the United States District Court at Richmond, Virginia.

During the questioning of the Chief Justice, a curious and interesting incident occurred. Vice President Burr had been exceedingly careful, meticulously correct, and eminently impartial in every detail of the somewhat involved proceedings. He had ruled the conduct of the trial so that contending counsel had no complaints and so that each witness was properly examined. Evidently he considered that certain questions presented to the Chief Justice had not been worded so as to bring out the pertinent facts. Consequently, the Vice President supplemented the questions of the House managers by making further inquiries while Marshall was on the witness stand. This proof of Burr's insistence upon a full presentation of available evidence did not pass unnoticed in the mind of the Chief Justice.

On February 13, the progress of the trial was interrupted while another matter of official business claimed the attention of the Congress. The votes of the members of the Electoral College were opened and counted under the direction of the Vice President. For the first time, this ceremony was conducted in public, with crowded galleries. Also for the first time, the electors had cast separate ballots for President and for Vice President. This was in compliance with the Twelfth Amendment to the Constitution, which had been adopted since the preceding presidential election. With no apparent show of emotion, Aaron Burr, in his official position as President of the

Senate, announced that Thomas Jefferson and George Clinton
had been duly elected to the respective positions of President
and Vice President of the United States.

Then the trial was resumed, and proceeded until the end of
February. On March 1, 1805, they were ready to vote. There
was a great crowd at the Capitol on that day, and the vote was
taken amid a scene of suppressed excitement and solemn adher-
ence to established forms of procedure.

At last it would be seen whether or not the President's new
interpretation of impeachment would be upheld by two-thirds
of the Senators—23 votes would be needed against Associate
Justice Chase in order to remove him. The party alignment was
25 Republicans and 9 Federalists. Every Senator was present.
Even Senator Uriah Tracy of Connecticut, who was ill, was
carried into the room on a litter.

They voted on each article of impeachment separately. On
the first article, the result was 18 "Not guilty" and 16 "Guilty."
Nine Republican Senators had voted with the nine Federalists.
The party line had been broken: most amazing of all was the
fact that Senator Giles—Jefferson's hand-picked representative—
had voted "Not guilty"!

As each succeeding article was voted upon, it became apparent that the break in Jefferson's party following was consistent.
There were a few Senators who voted "Guilty" for this article
and "Not guilty" for that one, but on no article was the prosecution securing the 23 votes required to remove the Justice from
the supreme bench.

The article that seemed most likely to prevail against Justice
Chase was the eighth, the one accusing him of introducing purely
partisan politics into his charge to the Grand Jury in Baltimore
in 1803. On that, the vote was 15 "Not Guilty" and 19 "Guilty."
But 23 votes were necessary for a conviction!

When the voting was finished and the results had been veri-
fied, to prevent any future dispute, it was seen that the 19 votes
to convict on Article 8 were the greatest strength that the
Administration forces had been able to muster on any of the

decisions. The Vice President arose from his place on the rostrum and solemnly declared that Associate Justice Samuel Chase had been duly acquitted of all the charges that had been lodged against him by the House of Representatives, and that the charges therefore were dismissed.

Jefferson had failed in his attempt to secure control over the federal judiciary. He also had definitely lost his dictatorial control over the Republican Party.

Marshall and his Associate Justices on the Supreme Court had been guaranteed, by this result, full freedom from political intimidation in arriving at their decisions. No longer would they live and serve in fear of removal and disgrace if they happened, by the course of their decisions, to displease the party in power.

Randolph and Nicholson were stung to the quick by their defeat in the Senate. They rushed back to the House, after the verdict was rendered, and each of them proposed a new amendment to the Federal Constitution. Randolph's proposal provided for the removal of federal judges upon the joint action of the President and the two houses of Congress. Nicholson's proposal provided for the recall of United States Senators by the legislatures of their respective states. Neither proposal was ever put to a vote.

And the Vice President, who had been granted one brief month of power, of flattery, of attention such as few Vice Presidents ever have experienced—what of him? He was left to bow out of the picture, urbanely and gracefully, with the knowledge that he had handled a difficult role in a manner that reflected honor upon "himself, the Senate, and the Nation."

Immediately after the conclusion of the trial, the Senate ratified the nominations of three of the Vice President's relatives and friends to positions in the Louisiana Territory. These were the nominations of Judge Prevost, Dr. Brown, and General Wilkinson. But for Aaron Burr himself, there was no nomination.

The whispered rumors of a Cabinet post or a diplomatic mission to another country did not materialize after Colonel Burr had scuttled President Jefferson's carefully planned scheme to remove the Federalists from the Supreme Court and to bring that tribunal under the control of the executive branch of the government.

On March 2, 1805, the Senate of the United States was in executive session. Vice President Burr was presiding. At a lull in the proceedings, he arose and announced that he now would take leave of his position. Instantly, every member of the Senate was alert. There were in the atmosphere those elements of surprise, suspense, wonder, and expectation that presage the imminence of a great event.

While they sat silent and watched and listened, Aaron Burr stood and spoke to the Senators, extemporaneously. No one took note of the passage of time; after he had concluded his remarks, no one seemed to know how long he had spoken. There were no stenographic reports in those days, but in part, the retiring Vice President said:

> I now challenge your attention to considerations more momentous than any which regard merely your personal honor and character—the preservation of law, of liberty, and of the Constitution.
>
> This house, I need not remind you, is a sanctuary, a citadel of law, of order, and of liberty; it is here, in this exalted refuge—here, if anywhere, that resistance will be made to the storms of political frenzy, and the silent arts of corruption; and if the Constitution be destined ever to perish by the sacrilegious hands of the demagogue or the usurper, which God avert, its expiring agonies will be on this floor.
>
> I now must bid you farewell. It probably is a final separation, a dissolution perhaps forever, of those associations, which I hope have been mutually satisfactory. I would console myself, and you, however, with the reflection that though we are separated, we shall be engaged in the common

cause of disseminating the principles of freedom
and social order.

I always shall regard the proceedings of this
body with interest and solicitude. I shall feel for its
honor and for the national honor so intimately con-
nected with it.

And now I take my leave of you, with expres-
sions of personal respect and with my prayers and
good wishes for you.

It is reported that his farewell address, delivered under
dramatic circumstances, was the greatest oration that has ever
been delivered in the Senate of the United States. Certain it
is that no other speech in either house of Congress ever produced the emotional results caused by this one. Some Senators
confessed in their letters and diaries that they did not regain
their usual composure till quite some time afterward. After the
Vice President had descended from the rostrum, after he had
walked down the aisle, after he had passed through the door,
after the door had closed and he no longer was with them,
there was a period of some fifteen minutes when the Senate was
in session but with no presiding officer. No one seemed willing
to break the spell that had been cast over them. Finally, the
president pro tempore took the chair and work was resumed.

Then they approved a measure giving Colonel Burr the
franking privilege for life—but the House did not have time to
act upon it before the close of the session.

They also passed a resolution, unanimously, to the effect "that
the thanks of the Senate be presented to Aaron Burr, as testimony of the impartiality and ability with which he has presided
over their deliberations, and of their entire approbation of his
conduct in the discharge of the arduous and important duties
assigned to him as President of the Senate."

ADDITIONAL REFERENCES

Annals of Congress, 1801-1805. Washington, D.C.: Gales and Seaton, 1801-5.

Biddle, Charles. *The Autobiography of Charles Biddle.* Philadelphia: E. Claxton and Company, 1883.

Brown, Everett Somerville, ed. *William Plumer's Memorandum of Proceedings in the United States Senate, 1803-1807.* New York: The Macmillan Co., 1923.

Jay, William. *The Life of John Jay,* 2 vols. New York: J. & J. Harper, 1833.

Pellow, George. *John Jay.* Boston: Houghton Mifflin Co., 1890.

Trumbull, John. *Autobiography, Reminiscences of John Trumbull.* New York and London: Wylie and Putnam; New Haven: B. L. Hamlen, 1841.

CHAPTER IX

The Western Expedition

AARON BURR should be known in our history as the American Phoenix because he repeatedly arose from the ashes of defeat to embark again upon the road which he believed would lead him toward some new success. He was not willing to accept any defeat as a final decision against him.

When he left the vice-presidency in March, 1805, it certainly appeared to his enemies that he was ruined politically, socially, and financially. They did not expect him to attain any further position of prominence, in any field.

It was during his term as Vice President, however, that the United States Senate had ratified the treaty with France which made the Louisiana Purchase a reality. Both Kentucky and Tennessee had been admitted to the Union while he was a member of the United States Senate. He had presided over the Senate when Ohio was admitted to the Union as the seventeenth state. Jefferson himself had directed Burr's attention to the new western country by the belated appointments of Prevost, Brown, and Wilkinson.

What was more natural, then, than that Colonel Burr should see in the Louisiana Territory the basis for his return to the national political scene?

As soon as his vice-presidency came to a close, he made a leisurely trip to New Orleans and returned to the East again. He left Philadelphia on April 10, 1805, reached New Orleans on June 25, and did not arrive back in Washington until late in November of that same year.

With several traveling companions, he proceeded on horse-back from Philadelphia to Pittsburgh. There, he purchased "a floating edifice" for the trip down the Ohio and Mississippi Rivers to New Orleans. It was a houseboat, sixty feet long and fourteen feet wide. It had a living-dining room, a kitchen, and two bedrooms. There was a fireplace in the living room and one in the kitchen. There was glass in the windows and steps leading to a walk the full length of the roof. Of course, a crew of several persons was employed to manage the boat and to prepare meals.

It should be noted that Colonel Burr's trip from the East to New Orleans and return was something of an exploit in itself. Few men in his position would have undertaken it; getting to New Orleans by boat, on the great rivers (the Ohio and the Mississippi), was one thing—returning over "the Trace" from Natchez to Nashville was quite another.

Some military work had been done to construct a road through the wilderness in 1802 and 1803. But it had been a half-hearted attempt and the forces of nature had quickly regained their dominance.

Colonel Burr made the trip in July, 1805, when the summer weather prevailed. There were numberless mosquitoes and swarms of flies. Poisonous snakes and large alligators were numerous in the swamps and streams. Many travelers were robbed by bandits and some (who resisted) were killed in cold blood.

Yet in his letters to Theodosia there was no word of complaint. Evidently the former Vice President took the adverse conditions as matters of course. Perhaps the physical discomforts were hardly noticed; in his mind plans for the future were taking shape, and along with them were thoughts of the exquisitely beautiful Madeline Price (the Maid of Half-Way Hill), whom he had met while a guest of Colonel Osmun at Windy Hill Manor, just outside Natchez.

During the progress of this trip, Colonel Burr met and talked with many people in all walks of life. Among the more prominent were Harman and Margaret Blennerhassett, Jonathan Dayton (former Senator from New Jersey), John Smith (the Ohio Senator), Henry Clay, Matthew Lyon (former member of Congress from Vermont), John Brown (the Kentucky Senator), General John Adair (the other Senator from Kentucky), General Andrew Jackson, General James Wilkinson, "General" William Eaton, Daniel Clark (perhaps the most wealthy merchant of that era in New Orleans), John Watkins (Mayor of New Orleans), Casa Calvo (the Spanish Commissioner in New Orleans), James Workman (Judge of the Parish Court), and Edward Livingston (a representative of the U.S. government). Of course he visited with his stepson, John Bartow Prevost, now holding his appointment as a federal judge in New Orleans, and he was guest of honor at the Convent of the Ursuline Nuns in New Orleans.

Everywhere in the West, he was received with cordiality. Balls and banquets were held in his honor. From the standpoint of excitement, honor, and glory, no experience could have been more rewarding. Social and political leaders vied with one another to entertain him.

At Nashville, he was the house guest of General Andrew Jackson at The Hermitage. In the town itself there was a parade preceding a banquet at which he was the guest of honor.

At Natchez, he was the center of attention at a series of parties in the great houses that had been built by the wealthy planters of the area.

But if his reception had been cordial in Lexington, Cincinnati, Nashville, and Natchez, it was even more flattering in New Orleans. To the people of New Orleans, Colonel Burr was the one great man who understood their position, their needs, and their problems. Again there were parades, parties, and gala balls. The Colonel was called upon to make a speech after a testimonial banquet at which he was given the keys to the city.

From mid-November, 1805, when he returned to the East across the mountain barrier, until mid-August, 1806, when he arrived in Pittsburgh on his second western trip, Colonel Burr was regarded as a national hero throughout the western country. The people of the West, no matter what their party politics might be, believed that he would become the dynamic leader

in the inevitable war with Spain. They considered him to be
the potential liberator of the Floridas, Texas, and even Mexico.
This war, which was so sure to come, would relieve the western
parts of the United States from the repeated threats and pressures from "the Dons." Colonel Burr was to be the instrument
of America's manifest destiny to expand until it would reach
the shores of the Pacific Ocean.

In all of this, there was no hint of any disloyalty to the
United States. In no way, either in private conversations or in
public statements, did Colonel Burr indicate any deviation from
his loyalty to his country.

In the East, however, all sorts of rumors were being circulated about his journey and about the motives for it. Portents
of future trouble soon became apparent. His enemies were using
every opportunity to present his trip as having questionable
overtones.

Leading politicians in New York and Virginia were aghast
when news of Colonel Burr's favorable reception was received
from the West. What would come of this resurgence of honor
and glory for the man whom they had considered to have been
removed from the political scene? Would Burr have to be dealt
with all over again? At any rate, he would have to be watched;
his motives would have to be made to look questionable. The
public would have to be inflamed against him. No matter what
he might do, it would have to have the label of wrongdoing
attached to it. Every gesture that he might make was to be made
a reason for suspicion.

Otherwise, this man would again occupy a seat in the United
States Senate—from one of the western states—he might even
aspire to the presidency again!

Burr was starting to live his political life over again! Had
he not already organized the Indiana Canal Company, with a
charter just like that of The Manhattan Company, so that it
could establish its own bank? Had he not been negotiating for
land again, somewhere in Louisiana?

So in the East ugly rumors were circulated by his enemies.
Anything that was anti-Burr was rushed into print and put before

the public. He must be stopped before he could achieve another success. Those who were in positions of power were determined to keep his star from rising once more above the horizon.

Evidently one of the things which the trip served to impress on Colonel Burr's mind was the notion that war with Spain was inevitable, and that it was imminent. Practically everyone whom he met on his trip had expressed such beliefs. General Wilkinson had indicated that the war could start at any time, upon a signal from him.*

As a consequence, Colonel Burr now considered that he had two strings to his western bow, one military and one political. If war was sure to come, he might yet wear a general's insignia and become a military hero as the leader of a group of Americans who might liberate Mexico from Spain. If it could be that no war might develop, he still could establish a new American state in the Louisiana Territory and serve either as its Governor or as one of its United States Senators in Washington.

After his return to the East, and as his plans began to take shape and to crystallize into definite form, Colonel Burr conferred with two foreign diplomats who represented their nations in Washington. These were the Honorable Anthony Merry, Minister from Great Britain, and the Marquis Don Carlos Martínez de Yrujo, Minister from Spain. Neither of these men made any definite committments on behalf of their governments, but they did make reports concerning their conversations with Colonel Burr.

Colonel Burr's plans for his activities in the Louisiana Territory, and particularly in the Ouachita region, never were reduced to a definitive written statement. It is claimed by some historians that he described his plans differently on different occasions and to different individuals. Whether this be true or

---

* Concerning the likelihood of war with Spain over the boundaries of Louisiana and related matters, see appropriate sections of the messages of President Jefferson to Congress, as follows: The Fifth Annual Message (December 3, 1805), The Sixth Annual Message (December 2, 1806), and the Seventh Annual Message (October 27, 1807).

not, there can be no doubt that he did plan an expedition to the West.

Before the final die was cast in favor of the western expedition, the former Vice President considered it desirable to hold one more conversation with Mr. Jefferson. He was received at the White House on February 22, 1806. It was apparent, as a result of what transpired at this meeting, that the President intended to force his former associate and running mate to work out his own salvation. It was an absolute fact that Mr. Jefferson would recommend no federal appointment of any kind for Colonel Burr. There was no chance for a Cabinet post, no army commission, no place in the diplomatic service. When the conference ended, both men had this understanding and Jefferson recorded it in his diary.

As a result of the purely negative attitude taken by President Jefferson in the situation, Colonel Burr saw only one possible avenue for the rebuilding of his political career. The East was closed to him, but there most certainly was opportunity in the West. He decided to proceed with his plans. He would lead a band of adventurous colonists to a desirable section of the Louisiana Territory. There he would establish a new state and await the outbreak of warfare—that warfare which now appeared certain to develop between the United States and the Spanish government of Mexico.

As a means toward achieving such ends, Colonel Burr arranged to purchase from Colonel Charles Lynch about 400,000 acres of land in what had been the Bastrop Grant* on the Ouachita River. The location of the Bastrop Grant was exactly

---

* Baron Bastrop had been born in 1759 in Holland, and his original name was Philip Hendrick Nering Bogel. About 1800 he changed his name to Philipe Enrique Neri, el Baron de Bastrop. Apparently this change was recognized by the Spanish Crown. He secured a huge grant of Louisiana land, with the understanding that he would recruit colonists to settle parts of it. An established community on the Ouachita River was considered to be desirable, from the Spanish viewpoint, when all of Louisiana was Spanish territory. The Baron did persuade some adventurous souls to establish homes on certain parts of this land. Other parts were sold or traded. In the course of his land manipulations, the Baron became indebted

suited to Colonel Burr's needs. From reports that he had received, it appeared that the ground was fertile, that some of the streams would provide water power, and that the climate was favorable. Consequently, it provided a good place for the settlement of families from the East. It could serve as the location for a new state (the state of Burrsylvania) in the American Union. It also was true that the region was close to the border between the American and Spanish territory. Consequently, it would provide an ideal base from which to conduct a military expedition into Mexico.

After the February interview with Jefferson, the full attention of the former Vice President was directed toward forming and leading an expedition to these western lands. Funds were raised or pledged. A staff was appointed. Flatboats were built; supplies were collected; volunteers were recruited; maps were copied; plans were made. There was much activity, involving a considerable number of people.

While all this was being done, blindly biased opposition by those who desired to keep Aaron Burr from a position of power was being fanned into a consuming flame. Even as the expedition was just beginning to take definite form, Colonel Burr was required to appear in court, on two different occasions, in Kentucky. In both of the proceedings against him, no testimony worthy of the name was presented to show that his plans were illegal in any way. No decision was rendered against him.

Among those who appeared in the courtroom, either to assist in the defense of Colonel Burr or to indicate by their presence that they had faith in the acceptable nature of his plans, was Henry Clay. Though still a young man, Clay already had established his reputation as a gifted lawyer and as a man of the highest moral principles. He took part in the Burr defense,

---

to Edward Livingston (who had moved from New York to New Orleans) and to several other Americans. In order to clear his records and to secure funds, he transferred certain land titles to Judge (Col.) Charles Lynch of Kentucky, subject to a settlement with Livingston. He then left Louisiana and went to Texas. It was the Lynch part of the Bastrop Grant that Colonel Burr bought, and the purchase price included $30,000 to be paid to Livingston as well as $5,000 (perhaps more) to Judge Lynch.

opposing the Federalist Attorney General of Kentucky, Joseph Hamilton Daveiss.* He did this only after having secured the personal assurance of the former Vice President that he contemplated no program that would be adverse to the welfare and the territorial integrity of the United States.

One of Colonel Burr's chief advisers concerning the expedition was General James Wilkinson. Wilkinson had been a young officer in the War of the Revolution and Burr had made his acquaintance then. He had remained in the military service and had become the highest-ranking officer in the United States Army. At the same time, as a result of his reputed friendship with Colonel Burr, he had been appointed to serve as the civil Governor of Louisiana Territory. Wilkinson's military headquarters were at New Orleans, and it was he who was directing the conduct of American affairs along the troubled and disputed border with Mexico.

Colonel Burr had kept General Wilkinson advised as to the progress of his expedition, using cipher or code letters for this purpose. There was nothing unusual about such a method; many men of prominence in the colonial and early nationalist periods used private codes for their correspondence. Such a procedure protected messages from the prying eyes of the curious, in an era when letters might be opened and read by almost anyone who handled them.

Colonel Burr assumed that General Wilkinson was loyal to the government of the United States and that he was a man of honor who could be trusted. He did not know that Wilkinson had entered into certain secret agreements with the Spanish government, through the viceroyalty of Mexico. He did not realize that Wilkinson was accepting pay from both the American and the Spanish governments and that he had to play a very clever part in order to maintain his equivocal position.

It was Wilkinson, acting to preserve his own power and prestige, who led President Jefferson to see the possibility of

---

* Daveiss was a rabid Federalist. He himself had added "Hamilton" to his name.

charging Colonel Burr with treason. After making certain altera-
tions in Burr's code letter of July 29, 1806, he forwarded that
document, together with an alarming report of his own, to
Jefferson.

By means of this maneuver, Wilkinson provided the means
for removing Burr from the scene in the Southwest while making himself more secure with both the American administration
in Washington and the Spanish administration in Mexico City.
Not only did his act provide certain ruin for Colonel Burr's
expedition; it even seemed to promise the death penalty for
Colonel Burr himself. Burr would be executed: he never would
rise again.

While General Wilkinson was writing inflammatory reports
to President Jefferson and setting a trap for Colonel Burr in
Mississippi and Louisiana, Burr was hurrying his plans for the
expedition. The first group of colonists for Burrsylvania started
down the Ohio River in December, 1806, and reached Bayou
Pierre, above Natchez, on January 11, 1807.

It was at this point that the expedition collapsed. Stirred into
action by reports from Wilkinson and other agents, Jefferson
had issued a Presidential Manifesto (November 27, 1806) against
Burr and his associates.* Soon afterward, New Orleans was
placed under martial law and all of the towns along the Mississippi were alerted to prepare for possible trouble.

At Bayou Pierre and at the mouth of Cole's Creek, Colonel
Burr was interviewed by representatives of the territorial government of Mississippi, and he was required to appear before
a grand jury at Washington, Mississippi, then the territorial
capital. This grand jury found nothing illegal or treasonable in
his activities. It did direct its criticisms toward Colonel Burr's
accusers, and it condemned their methods and their procedures.
General Wilkinson's tactics were cited with disfavor.

A great manhunt had been launched from the national capi-

---

* The exact wording of this manifesto, or proclamation, issued by
President Jefferson, deserves careful study. It was designed to indicate that
some person or persons (obviously Colonel Burr and his associates) were
guilty, before any trial had taken place.

tal, however, and the territorial grand jury was unable to make its decisions effective. Jefferson, his followers, and his appointees were determined that Colonel Burr's career should end at this point. They were ready to assert that he was guilty of a capital crime, even before he was brought to trial on the charges.

Colonel Burr's reaction to the situation in Mississippi was to disband his expedition. He then left Natchez on horseback, riding toward the East with only one companion.

There has been some speculation among certain writers and historians to the effect that he intended to go to settlements on the Tombigbee River, and start a new expedition aimed at seizing control of the Floridas, both East and West. Such a decision on his part seems most unlikely, however, for now he had no men, no supplies, and no financial backing for such an idea.

It is much more reasonable to assume that he rode eastward in order to reach South Carolina, so that he could rest and recuperate at the Alston home while determining what future course to follow.

Before he had proceeded very far through the wilderness, he was arrested. His captors took him overland to Richmond, Virginia.

ADDITIONAL REFERENCES

Anon. *The Conspiracy of Col. Aaron Burr.* New York: G. W. Simmons, 1854.

Abernethy, Thomas P. *The Burr Conspiracy.* New York: Oxford University Press, 1954.

McCaleb, Walter F. *The Aaron Burr Conspiracy,* expanded ed., Intro. by Charles A. Beard. New York: Wilson-Erickson, Inc., 1936.

———. "Early Patterns for Tyranny in the U.S." *The Texas Quarterly,* Vol. II, No. 4 (Winter, 1959).

———. *New Light on Aaron Burr.* "The Texas Quarterly Studies"; Austin, Texas: University of Texas, 1963.

Stafford, William H. *The Blennerhassett Papers.* Cincinnati: Moore, Wilstach and Baldwin, 1864.

Thorning, Joseph F. *Miranda: World Citizen.* Gainesville, Florida: University of Florida Press, 1952. (Chapter XIV.)

CHAPTER X

The Trial for Treason

UPON his arrival in Richmond, Colonel Burr was held by the federal authorities for trial on the charge of treason. The investigation and the trial itself could have been conducted by Judge Cyrus Griffin of the U.S. Circuit Court, but Chief Justice John Marshall chose to be present and to preside, as was his right. It was an important action for him to take. No doubt when he took it, he remembered Colonel Aaron Burr's part in the trial of Associate Justice Samuel Chase.

Seldom has the city of Richmond experienced any public spectacle approaching the Burr trial in dramatic quality and in emotional appeal. The attention of the entire nation was focused upon the city and upon the cast of characters assembled there.

Chief among them was Colonel Burr himself. The city of Richmond received him well. Special arrangements were made to safeguard his health and to provide for his comfort. He secured a whole wardrobe of new clothing, and when he arrived in the courtroom he made a very favorable appearance. Throughout the course of the trial, he was the center of attention.

There also were Chief Justice John Marshall and his associate, Circuit Judge Griffin. The lawyers appointed by the government to prosecute the case were George Hay, William Wirt, and Alexander McRae. It is possible that the Attorney General of the United States, the Honorable Caesar Rodney, made several trips from Washington to Richmond to confer with the prosecuting attorneys. Colonel Burr directed his own defense and had associated with him Edmund Randolph, Charles Lee,

John Wickham, Benjamin Botts, John Baker, and Luther Martin.
The government assembled a group of more than one hundred
persons to serve as witnesses. They were headed by General
James Wilkinson, General William Eaton, Commodore Thomas
Truxton, Colonel George Morgan and the two laborers: Jacob
Allbright and Peter Taylor (one of the gardeners employed by
the Blennerhassetts). Harman Blennerhassett was in the
city, but his wife, Margaret, remained in the West, with
their children. General Andrew Jackson had been summoned
to testify against the defendant but never was called to
the witness stand. He stood on the steps of the Capitol and on
street corners, speaking in Colonel Burr's behalf. John Randolph
of Roanoke served as the foreman of the Grand Jury and Colonel
Edward Carrington was foreman of the trial jury. Both Senator
William Giles and Congressman Wilson C. Nicholas of Virginia
were summoned for jury duty, but both were challenged and
withdrew. Washington Irving was present as a newspaper cor-
respondent. Colonel Burr's chief lieutenants, other than his fellow lawyers, were Colonel Julien De Pestre, Erich Bollman, and
young Samuel Swartwout. Of course there were many others.
Unknown spectators came from every part of the country to see
and to hear until the city could accommodate no more visitors.
And to complete the amazing picture, there were General Joseph
Alston of South Carolina and his fascinating wife, Mrs. Theodosia Burr Alston. The social leaders of Richmond seized upon
the situation as an excellent excuse for a great series of receptions and parties.

One man who should have been physically present at this
gathering of notables in Richmond did not make his appearance.
Mr. Jefferson remained in Washington, eagerly dispatching
detailed instructions to Mr. Hay and anxiously reading the
bulletins that Hay sent back to him. Colonel Burr used the only
legal means within his command in order to have Mr. Jefferson
face him directly in court. On June 9, 1807, he requested the
Chief Justice to issue a *subpoena duces tecum* to the President
of the United States.

In an address to the court, while this request was being

considered, Luther Martin presented the following argument: "The President has undertaken to prejudge my client by declaring, that 'Of his guilt there can be no doubt.' He has assumed to himself the knowledge of the Supreme Being himself . . . He has proclaimed him a traitor in the face of that country, which has rewarded him. He has let slip the dogs of war, the hell-hounds of persecution, to hunt down my friend. And would this President of the United States, who has raised all this absurd clamour, pretend to keep back the papers which are wanted for this trial, where life itself is at stake? . . . Can it be presumed that the President would be sorry to have Colonel Burr's innocence proved?"

Of course the President angrily refused to appear in court or to submit the papers that were desired, and here again there was established a precedent that remains to this day.

The trials (there were several of them) were dramatic and spectacular. Beginning on May 22, 1807, they continued until October 20 of that year. Practically five months of continuous tension and excitement, with more sensational surprises than have ever marked any other trial, or series of trials, in American history—either before or since this one!

The prosecutors found that some of the witnesses whom they had brought to Richmond had no testimony to offer against Colonel Burr. Others, on the witness stand, invoked the provisions of the Fifth Amendment to the Constitution. Even though the government's attorneys had blank pardons, already signed by Jefferson, in their hands, they were unable to find anyone who could testify, under oath, that treasonable acts had taken place. General Wilkinson, the key man in the government's case, was made to admit that he had altered the Burr materials that he had sent to Jefferson, and he was quite thoroughly discredited before he left the witness stand. "General" Eaton admitted that his claim against the federal government—a claim which was questionable and which had been neglected—had been settled suddenly (after it appeared that he could offer testimony damaging to Burr) by the payment of ten thousand dollars. Sergeant Dunbaugh admitted that he had been AWOL but that this charge against him had been dropped when he agreed to be a witness for the government's case. The Blennerhassett laborers obviously had been rehearsed for their stories to be told on the stand and they became confused under cross-examination. It was no secret on the streets and in the taverns of Richmond that Mr. Hay, who was in charge of the prosecution, could provide money for all sorts of "expenses" for anyone who would give testimony against Colonel Burr.

The government was unable to prove its case, and Colonel Burr was declared to be "Not Guilty." The general public had been unduly inflamed against him, however, and after an interval, he decided to make an extended tour of Europe.

ADDITIONAL REFERENCES

Adams, Henry. *John Randolph*. Boston: Houghton, Mifflin Company, 1882.

Beirne, Francis F. *Cry Treason: The Trial of Aaron Burr*. New York: Hastings House, 1959.

Beveridge, Albert J. *The Life of John Marshall*, 4 vols. Boston: Houghton Mifflin Company, 1919.

Coombe, J. J. *The Trial of Aaron Burr*. Washington, D.C.: Wm. H. and O. H. Morrison, 1864.

Robertson, David. *Reports of the Trials of Colonel Aaron Burr*, 2 vols. Philadelphia: Hopkins and Earle, 1808.

Tracy, John E. "The Trial of Aaron Burr." *Michigan Alumnus*, Vol. LVI, No. 10 (December 3, 1949).

CHAPTER XI

Four Years in Europe

FROM June 7, 1808, until June 7, 1812, Colonel Aaron Burr was on a trip of Odyssean proportions. From New York City, where he took leave of Theodosia, he went to Halifax, Nova Scotia, where he visited Sir George Prevost, an uncle of his two stepsons. Then he proceeded to England and remained there for nine months. He was the house guest of the philosopher and economist Jeremy Bentham in London during much of this time. He also was welcomed and regarded practically as a relative by various members of the Prevost family. His stay in London was broken by leisurely trips to Oxford, Birmingham, Liverpool, and several other British cities.

He derived special satisfaction from a brief visit to Scotland, for he was entertained by a number of prominent people in Edinburgh and several receptions were arranged in his honor.

His period of residence in Great Britain was not without its difficulties, however; certain members of the American diplomatic and consular staffs in London (appointees of President Jefferson) raised questions about his status. As a result of this, he became the subject of annoying surveillance. At first he tried to disregard this difficulty, but in time it had to be recognized and dealt with.

One of his activities, during his European travels, was the keeping of a private journal or diary. His original reason for doing this was to provide a basis from which he could tell Theodosia and her family about his trip. The journal was not intended for publication. Nor was it ever intended to be read literally.

Almost from the time of his arrival in England, Colonel Burr knew that he was being watched by secret agents, paid by his enemies. As a result, he intentionally placed in the journal various obscure statements, unusual abbreviations, strange mixtures of several languages, and matters of an allegorical nature. He found that it was expedient to omit entries that involved political questions and matters of international relations.

The events of April 4, 1809, give ample evidence for accepting such an opinion about the material in the journal. On that day, British government agents, apparently acting at the suggestion of representatives of the United States government, broke into his quarters and confiscated all of his books, papers, and documents. Later, after they had been searched and read, these things were returned to him, but after that incident, Colonel Burr felt that his possessions were never safe. From time to time, mysterious persons opened his mail before it reached him. And it is quite possible that unknown "visitors" reported to Americans in high places the things that the Colonel was writing in his journal.

In time, it became clear that it would be desirable for him to leave Great Britain and visit some other country. It was the Swedish Minister to Great Britain who suggested that he might go to Sweden. At the minister's request, passports were issued for Colonel Burr, his personal secretary, William Hosack, and the secretary's friend, Mr. Robinson.

At eight o'clock on the evening of April 24, 1809, His Britannic Majesty's packet *The Diana*, a sloop of only sixty tons, left Harwich bound for Gothenburg (Göteborg), Sweden. Aaron Burr was one of the passengers.

Although the American republic had existed as a nation for thirty-three years, no provision had yet been made for exchange of diplomatic representatives between the governments of Sweden and the United States. Colonel Burr's passport to the Scandinavian country had been secured through Baron de Brinkman, the Swedish Minister to Great Britain. Never before had any person who had held such high office in America visited Sweden.

Colonel Burr had chosen two books to read during the voyage from England to Sweden: Mary Wollstonecraft's account of her Swedish tour and the story of Sheridan's Revolution of 1772. In addition to his reading, he passed the time playing chess with another passenger who was a captain of the Swedish navy and in conversation with other passengers on the packet.

The Diana reached Gothenberg on the morning of May 3. The passengers transferred to a small boat and went to the customhouse. None of them had any difficulty in passing the customs inspection, but there was a complication at this point, none the less, for one of Colonel Burr's large trunks, containing his clothing, could not be found. Neither could some of his private papers be located.

The Colonel rented a three-room apartment in the home of a prosperous Swedish family, none of whom spoke any English or French.

The following day, he found that there was an American Consul in Gothenburg, a Mr. Smith. This Consul had a Swedish butler, or manservant, and the story of the missing trunk and document books was explained to him. About twenty-four hours later, this servant found both of the missing objects—still in the hold of the packet ship *Diana*.

The Colonel's secretary, William Hosack, had not accompanied him on *The Diana* but had remained in England to take care of certain business affairs. He arrived on another ship which reached Gothenburg on May 6. Both of them left the port city on the following day as the guests of a Swedish citizen named Mr. Hedborn who had his own carriage and horses. They arrived in Stockholm on the morning of May 11.

After arranging for living quarters for himself, his secretary, and Mr. Hosack's friend, Mr. Robinson—and a suitable place to hang Theodosia's portrait—the Colonel lost no time in using the letters of introduction that had been given to him in England.

One of these was from a Swedish Consul, Hendrik Gahn, addressed to General Carl Gahn of Colquhon. Another was from Colonel Mosheim, addressed to Baron Munck of Fulkila. A third, written by Baron de Brinkman, was addressed to Baron (General) Gustaf Armfelt. All three of these were delivered in person by the Colonel on May 12 and on the 13th a fourth letter was delivered to a banker named Mr. Wennerquist. As a result of these and of other contacts, the former Vice President of the United States gained a favored place in the upper social circle of the Swedish capital.

In his journal, he states that he was taken to a private club of The Society of Nobles, where his name was inscribed on the register and where he was made an honorary member.

Recent research indicates that this may have been The Society of the House of Bonde, which was a flourishing aristocratic city club at that time, and which has become the present-day Rosenbad.

Colonel Burr had learned enough Swedish for use in polite and utilitarian conversation as soon as he landed in Gothenburg. Now he spent his time in studying Sweden's history and her laws; he attended the theater; he visited famous buildings, galleries, and museums. Throughout all of it, he constantly was meeting new people. For a traveler in a strange country, he soon had a large circle of friends.

On May 17, 1809, he received notice that he was to be presented at Court, and when the notification arrived, it seemed to indicate that his presentation was to take place on that very day, without any time to secure a proper court costume. After some confusion, it developed that the royal levee would be held on June 1. On that day, the former Vice President, wearing a Spanish-type cloak, knee breeches, silver shoe buckles, a dress sword, and a three-cornered hat, was presented to the Regent and the Court by Baron Armfelt.

This Regent was recognized as King Charles XIII, but at this time his assumption of the kingly title was still being questioned in Sweden. King Gustavus IV, who had lost Finland to the Russians in 1808, had been arrested in France by General Klingspor and had been forced to abdicate. The new King (or

Regent) to whom Colonel Burr was presented, and with whom he conversed in French, was Gustavus' uncle.

On June 9, 1809, Colonel Burr was among those present at another court affair, and he was welcomed at the royal palace on other occasions for which no exact dates were recorded.

The former Vice President was an eligible widower at this time. He was fifty-two years old but looked younger. Although he was a small man in stature, he had a military carriage. His natural physical movements were quick, precise, and graceful. He seemed to be at home in any company and was noted for his ability as a conversationalist. There can be no doubt about his sincere interest in law, history, politics, military science, and the fine arts. With such a background, he was considered as a possible husband for more than one Swedish heiress, even though his own financial fortunes were at a low ebb.

The court ladies and society belles of Stockholm were not unmindful of the personal charm of this visiting American, who had held such a high place in the government of his own country.

On June 30, Colonel Burr was among those present when the Prince Regent was crowned as King Charles XIII. On July 14, official copies of the coronation medals were presented to him by the Director of the royal mint.

As the summer advanced, he followed, with keen interest, the maneuvers of the Swedish, Danish, Russian, and French armies as news of their movements reached him from various sources. He visited Upsala, Gripsholm, and other Swedish cities.

He became a friend and patron of the portrait painter, Carl Fredrik von Breda. It was in Breda's private gallery that the Colonel's portrait of Theodosia was on display.

For a time he offered advice to the people who were preparing the hollow logs used in draining a lake. He had had practical experience in this field through the use of hollow logs as water mains by The Manhattan Company, in New York City.

This summer of 1809 was one of the most pleasant and enjoyable interludes in all of Colonel Burr's exciting and active life.

It seems unfortunate that his Swedish vacation period was brought to a close at a time when his finest qualities and best potentialities were attracting favorable attention in high places.

A summer vacation was not just what the Colonel wanted. He was becoming restless. He still was dominated by his dream of becoming the liberator and perhaps the ruler of Mexico. This desire had provided a part of the motive for his western expedition in the United States. While he was in Europe, he continued to mention it in his letters to Theodosia. Apparently it served to obscure other opportunities for preferment that were before him in Europe.

The visit to Sweden came to a close on October 21, 1809, when Colonel Burr left through the port of Gothenburg (the same port at which he had arrived on May 3), en route to Elsinore, in the Kingdom of Denmark. He had been in Sweden for five months and eighteen days. Judging from his own record, this visit to Sweden provided a time for thinking and planning, preceding one final attempt to find backing for a military expedition into Mexico.

While crossing the Kingdom of Denmark, he traveled in his own carriage drawn by a pair of fine horses. With him were a coachman-valet, his secretary, and two personal friends. On November 8, he reached Altona, near Hamburg in Germany. In several of the small German states, he was entertained by the reigning dukes or grand dukes. Even though his visits to these centers of culture and social activity were fascinating experiences, he stayed only a short time at each ducal Court. The dream of securing military aid to support a Mexican expedition still served as a lodestone, attracting him toward France.

During his visit in Göttingen, he heard that the Emperor Napoleon would look with favor upon the independence of Mexico and the other Spanish-American colonies. At once he curtailed his travel plans and made every effort to reach Paris quickly.

Once in the French capital, he contacted many representatives of Napoleon's imperial government. He wrote a number of proposals for aggressive action in Mexico and in Florida.

These were given some consideration while Spain was regarded as a hostile power. It was not very long, however, until Napoleon's armies overran Spain, and Joseph Bonaparte, the Emperor's brother, was proclaimed King of Spain. Of course this meant that he was King of the Spanish dominions overseas also. Naturally, Napoleon and his ministers would not grant Colonel Burr any promise of military or financial aid in securing the liberation of any Spanish territory in America, under these new circumstances. Nor did the Emperor want him to leave France in order to seek support elsewhere for a military campaign that might involve Mexico. In this point of view, the American Minister to the French Court concurred. Both the French and the American officials were in agreement to the effect that the best place for the former Vice President was within the Empire of France.

Colonel Burr's art protégé, John Vanderlyn, was living in Paris at this period. The two men were on friendly terms with one another, and for a brief time the Colonel lived at the Vanderlyn studio-apartment. They talked of art and of music, of money and of politics. They strolled along the boulevards and attended teas and receptions together.

Colonel Burr's old interest in the Holland Land Company revived during his residence in Europe. From Paris, he managed to make one or two trips to Amsterdam, where he met with the directors whose company controlled considerable tracts of land in New York State. It appears that his conferences proved to be somewhat less than satisfactory. His confidence in the financial possibilities were such, however, that he purchased an additional block of their stock.

Now that the possibility of French aid in the Mexican venture had vanished into thin air, while Joseph Bonaparte served as King of Spain, Colonel Burr began to give favorable attention to Theodosia's advice. For some time she had been urging him, in her letters, to return to New York City and to resume his legal practice. But when he finally did apply for a passport and visa, all sorts of technical difficulties were put into his way. Week after week and month after month the members of the

American diplomatic mission in France and the French politicians combined their forces in order to spin out a seemingly endless amount of official red tape.

It was only through the direct personal influence of a friendly nobleman, who stood high in Napoleon's favor, that Colonel Burr finally secured a passport to leave France. Even then, the vessel on which he sailed was captured by the British and the whole troublesome procedure of securing clearances and passage had to be repeated again in London, and the passage money had to be paid a second time. His funds were very low at this point. He found it necessary to sell most of the diamond, garnet, and topaz jewelry that he had bought for Theodosia in Germany and in France. He also had to sell the bolts of cloth that he had bought in Paris, and the collection of coins (intended for use as a gift to his grandson) which he had secured in each country that he had visited, in order to raise the money for his necessary expenses.

Even though the Colonel considered that he now was reduced to poverty, his personal effects still filled fourteen boxes and trunks, which had to be hauled in a lighter to the boat on which he sailed from England to the United States. Included in some of the boxes were several sets of rare books, some documents of importance, and the manuscript copy of his private journal.

His hope for the future—the motive which now carried him forward in his planning—was centered in his grandson, Aaron Burr Alston. If success seemed elusive now, the path toward ultimate victory and triumph could be charted for that time when Theodosia's son would become an adult. Joseph Alston was helping to prepare the way by his activity in the political arena in South Carolina. With a former Vice President for a grandfather and a former Governor for a father, the boy should have a political tradition of no mean proportions to build upon. The boy surely could become a Senator or a Governor, and the position of President of the United States would not be an impossible goal for him.

There can be no doubt but that the Colonel's thoughts

centered chiefly about Theodosia and her son as he sailed back
to his native country.

ADDITIONAL REFERENCES

Burr, Aaron. *The Private Journal of Aaron Burr,* 2 vols. Ed. Matthew L.
Davis. New York: Harper & Brothers, 1838. (See also the "Bixby
Edition": 2 vols, ed. William H. Samson, publ. William K. Bixby;
Rochester, N.Y.: The Genesee Press, 1903.)

CHAPTER XII

Return to New York
and the Death of Theodosia

COLONEL BURR's return to New York City and the resumption of his professional work as a lawyer in June, 1812, were accepted as matters of course by most Americans of that era. As soon as his law office was opened, the waiting room was filled with prospective clients. No fewer than five hundred persons called on him during the course of the first day. Fees totaling more than $2,000 were collected during the first week. Almost at once it became necessary for the former Vice President to employ younger lawyers as assistants. One of these assistants was Nelson Chase, who later became the son-in-law of Mme Jumel.

Hardly had there been time for Colonel Burr to become re-established in his old surroundings and in his professional work when the two ultimate tragedies of his life struck him in rapid succession.

Theodosia wrote him in a grief-laden letter that the boy— his only grandchild—Aaron Burr Alston, in whom his high hopes for the future had been centered, had died on June 30 of a fever. It was a most cruel blow for it meant the end of the direct descent of their "Burr dynasty." But Theodosia remained, even though she was physically ill and emotionally disturbed.

Theodosia and her father had not met since June 7, 1808. Both of them now felt that they should have a visit with one another. Joseph Alston was serving as Governor of South Carolina and was required to stay within the state while serving in that office.

Theodosia therefore planned to travel alone to New York City. The overland trip, in the winter season, was considered to be too arduous for her, in her weakened physical condition. But Colonel Burr was not willing for her to travel alone. Therefore he asked Dr. Timothy Green to go to South Carolina to accompany his daughter on the voyage. Theodosia also was to bring her personal maid and one or two other servants with her.

On December 31, 1812, the party sailed from Georgetown, South Carolina, on the pilot boat *The Patriot*, Captain Overstocks commanding.

By this time, the United States was at war with England and British men-of-war were patrolling the coasts of Georgia and the Carolinas. Governor Alston had prepared an official letter addressed to the commanding officer of the British fleet, asking safe passage for his wife, because of her illness.

The Patriot was stopped by a British warship and the letter was effective; Captain Overstocks was allowed to proceed. This was on the morning of January 1, 1813.

On the night of January 1, 1813, a severe storm swept the seas off Cape Hatteras, and the following day the vessel on which Theodosia had taken passage came ashore at Nag's Head without passengers or crew. Colonel Burr in New York and Governor Alston in Charleston wrote to one another for news— but there was no news. When it finally became clear that Theodosia had been lost at sea, Colonel Burr said to his law associates: "By this blow, I am separated from the human race."

With Theodosia were lost also some ten or twelve boxes of original letters and documents that she had held for her father during his travels overseas. She also had with her most of the correspondence that had passed between them while he had been in England and France. These personal papers were irreplaceable. Their loss has made it impossible to refer to the original records covering various phases of Colonel Burr's life, particularly during the period from 1800 to 1812. The lack of these documents explains why the accounts rendered by the Colonel's enemies are practically the only ones that have been available for use by historians since his death.

After Aaron Burr Alston had died on June 30, 1812, after Theodosia had been lost at sea off Nag's Head on January 1, 1813, and after Joseph Alston had died on September 10, 1816, someone discovered a letter among the effects that Theodosia had left at The Oaks when she set sail for New York City. This letter had been written a number of years before these three tragic deaths had occurred. In a moment of foreboding, she had set forth some of her thoughts for her husband to read, in the event of her death. It was addressed to "My dear Husband," and it reads as follows:

Whether it is the effect of extreme debility and disordered nerves, or whether it is really presentiment, the existence of which I have often been told and always have doubted, I cannot tell: but something whispers to me that my end approaches. In vain I reason with myself: in vain I occupy my mind and seek to fix my attention on other subjects: there is about me that dreadful heaviness and sinking of the heart, that awful foreboding of which it is impossible to divest myself. . . .

To you, my beloved, I leave my child, the child of my bosom, who was once a part of myself, and from whom I shall shortly be separated by the cold grave. You love him now, henceforth love him for me also. And, oh, my husband, attend to this last prayer of a doting mother! Never, never listen to what any other person tells you of him. Be yourself his judge on all occasions. He has faults: see them and correct them yourself. Desist not an instant from your endeavors to secure his confidence. It is a work which requires as much uniformity of conduct as warmth of affection toward him.

I know, my beloved, that you can perceive what

is right on this subject, as on every other. . . . I feel
hurried and agitated. Death is not welcome to me:
I confess it is ever dreaded. You have made me
too fond of life. Adieu then, thou kind, thou tender
husband. Adieu, friend of my heart. May heaven
prosper you, and may we meet hereafter. Adieu,
perhaps we may never see each other again in this
world. You are away: I wished to hold you fast,
and prevent you from going this morning.

But He who is wisdom itself ordains events:
we must submit to them. Least of all should I mur-
mur. I on whom so many blessings have been
showered: whose days have been numbered by
bounties, who have had such a husband, such a
child, and such a father. Oh, pardon me, my God,
if I regret leaving these. I resign myself. Adieu
once more and for the last time, my beloved.
Speak of me often to our son. Let him love the
memory of his mother, and let him know he was
loved by her.

Your wife, your fond wife,

THEO.

Following the disappearance of Mrs. Alston, a number of
doubtful stories arose concerning her fate. Their very number
tends to discredit all of them.

It was reported that the crew of *The Patriot* had mutinied
and had killed the officers and the passengers. Another story was
that the pilot boat had been captured by pirates and that the
officers and passengers had been forced to walk the plank. Some
said that Theodosia had been rescued from the wreck of *The
Patriot* but that her mind had been deranged; this accounts for
"the mysterious stranger of Alexandria." It is more difficult to
account for the lady who appeared in Victoria, Texas.

When stories of the possibility of Theodosia's survival were

devoted companion. There is no reference or record of any sort to indicate that they were married, but from this union had been born a son, named Aaron Columbus Burr.

Colonel Burr arranged for this young man to come to America, and he arrived in New York City about 1827. He was placed in a private school and the Colonel supervised his educational program.*

One of his clients in the latter period of his life was John Jacob Astor, and another was Mme Stephen Jumel, both of whom made fortunes by their shrewd ability to judge real-estate values in New York City. Madame's son-in-law, Nelson Chase, became one of Aaron Burr's law partners. And on July 1, 1833, Madame Eliza Bowen Jumel was married to former Vice President Aaron Burr, by the Rev. Dr. David Bogart, a clergyman of the Dutch Reformed Church. The wedding took place in Madame's home, the imposing and historic Roger Morris mansion that had served as Washington's headquarters for a time during the War of the Revolution. On their wedding trip into Connecticut, they visited Aaron's friend John Trumbull in New Haven and they were lavishly entertained by Aaron's nephew, Governor Henry W. Edwards, at Hartford, Connecticut. Once more, social and political leaders responded to the magic that was in the name of Aaron Burr.

Madame was the wealthiest woman in New York at this time; perhaps she was the wealthiest woman in the United States. The value of her properties was estimated to be about three million dollars. Her age was fifty-six and the Colonel's was seventy-eight. Although each could have helped the other in many ways, the marriage that started so auspiciously soon was wrecked by quarrels over financial affairs. The amounts involved were relatively small, but they caused difficulties. After one of

---

* Aaron Columbus Burr married and had one son, Aaron Hippolite Burr, who died leaving no children. As has been indicated previously, Theodosia's only child died on June 30, 1812, at the age of ten years. Consequently, there are no direct descendants of Colonel Aaron Burr now living.

these altercations, Colonel Burr packed his trunks and moved out of his wife's big house.

For a time, after he left Madame's mansion, he lived with Aaron Columbus Burr, across the Hudson River in New Jersey. One day he suffered a slight stroke while at his law office and it was inadvisable for him to be taken to his son's home.

When the news reached Madame, she sent her coach and had him brought back to the mansion on Harlem Heights. Eliza and her corps of servants nursed him back to health again.

The Colonel and Madame spent happy days together while he was recuperating from the stroke, but new difficulties soon developed and she applied for a divorce—on the usual grounds in the State of New York.

When he first heard that his wife was instituting suit for divorce, the Colonel decided to turn the tables upon her. Consequently, he entered a countersuit, listing the same provocation which she charged against him. After some reflection upon the matter, he adopted a more chivalrous course of action, withdrawing his suit and offering no opposition to hers.

Following a hearing before Judge Philo Ruggles, the divorce was granted, and it would have become effective on September 14, 1836, but on that day, Colonel Aaron Burr died. After his death, Madame regarded herself as Colonel Burr's widow rather than as a divorcée. She continued to use his name, signing official documents "Eliza B. Burr."

During the final months of Colonel Burr's life, after his second separation from Madame, he had a comfortable apartment at Winant's Inn in Port Richmond, on Staten Island. He had one male servant and depended upon the personnel of the inn for various other services.

His apartment faced New York Harbor, so that the panorama of harbor traffic and the Manhattan skyline were available for him to observe. He received many visitors—prominent men in the fields of politics, banking, the arts, and the law; old friends; and relatives. He also received a large quantity of mail, including letters, books, and papers. He had excellent medical care and attention, but his strength gradually ebbed and on September 14, 1836, he died.

A simple funeral service was held in the inn parlors, conducted by the Rev. P. J. Van Pelt of the Dutch Reformed Church at Port Richmond.

Colonel Burr's body was transported to South Amboy by boat, then to Hightstown by roalroad, and finally to Princeton by a funeral carriage. The body lay in state, in the Chapel of Nassau Hall (erected by his father, the Rev. Aaron Burr), and an impressive service was held there on the afternoon of September 16, 1836. The order of service included:

> Prayer by the Rev. P. J. Van Pelt of Port Richmond
> Reading of the 90th Psalm
> Funeral Oration by the Rev. Dr. James Carnahan,
>   President of Princeton
> Prayer by the Rev. Dr. B. H. Rice of Princeton

There was a military guard of New Jersey troops (the Mercer Guards and others) and many members of the faculties of the college and the seminary were present. Practically the entire student body of the college and the seminary and many people from the town of Princeton joined in the solemn funeral procession to the burial ground. The body was buried in "President's Row," near the graves of his father (the Rev. Aaron Burr) and his grandfather (the Rev. Jonathan Edwards).

The pallbearers were General Robert Swartwout, General Bogardus, Colonel Romeyn, Colonel Scott, Colonel Samuel Swartwout, Major Popham, Mr. Western, and Mr. Corp.

A stone, to mark the grave, was made at Brown's Marble Yard in New York City, upon the order of Mr. Alfred Edwards (a cousin). The inscription reads:

AARON BURR

Born February 6, 1756
Died September 14, 1836

A Colonel in the Army of the Revolution
Vice President of the United States
from 1801 to 1805

Colonel Burr's last will and testament made disposition of
a number of leaseholds and various partial interests in certain
parcels of real estate and other property. The estate was not
finally settled until quite a number of years after his death.
When the settlement was made, one of his heirs received real
estate and other property worth approximately $10,000. Other
heirs received proportionally valuable bequests. His correspondence and documentary files that had accumulated after his
return from the European trip were given to Matthew L. Davis.
Mr. Davis destroyed some of the files, for reasons which are
unaccountable. Others were preserved and published, but they
form a fragmentary and unsatisfactory record of the many and
varied aspects of the life of a great man.

ADDITIONAL REFERENCES

"Burr, Aaron." *The Columbia Encyclopedia.* New York: Columbia University Press, 1950.

Burr, Samuel Engle Jr. "Mrs. Aaron Burr's Passport of 1853." *Autograph
Collectors' Journal,* Vol. III, No. 4 (Summer, 1951).

Hecht, Marie B., and Herbert S. Parmet. "New Light on Burr's Later
Life." *New York Historical Society Quarterly,* Vol. XLVII, No. 4 (October, 1963).

Todd, Charles Burr. *In Olde New York.* New York: The Grafton Press,
1907.

Tompkins, H. B. *A List of Books Relating to Aaron Burr.* Brooklyn, N.Y.:
Historical Printing Club, 1892.

APPENDIX A

Electoral Votes

THE U.S. ELECTIONS OF 1792, 1796, AND 1800

	CANDIDATES	PARTY	ELECTORAL VOTES CAST		
			1792	1796	1800
1.	George Washington	Federalist	132	2	0
2.	John Adams	Federalist	77	71	65
3.	Thomas Pinkney	Federalist	0	59	0
4.	Charles C. Pinkney	Federalist	0	1	64
5.	John Jay	Federalist	0	5	1
6.	Thomas Jefferson	Republican	4	68	73
7.	Aaron Burr	Republican	1	30	73
8.	George Clinton	Republican	50	7	0
9.	Samuel Adams	Federalist	0	15	0
10.	Oliver Ellsworth	Federalist	0	11	0
11.	James Iredell	Federalist	0	3	0
12.	Samuel Johnston	Federalist	0	2	0
13.	John Henry	Federalist	0	2	0
	Total Votes Cast		264	276	276

ELECTORAL VOTES FOR ADAMS
AND THE PINKNEYS

U. S. ELECTIONS OF 1796 AND 1800

STATE	JOHN ADAMS 1796	1800	CHANGE	PINKNEY (Thomas) 1796	PINKNEY (Charles C.) 1800	CHANGE
New Hampshire	6	6		0	6	+ 6
Vermont	4	4		4	4	
Massachusetts	16	16		13	16	+ 3
Rhode Island	4	4		0	3	+ 3
Connecticut	9	9		4	9	+ 5
New York	12	0	—12	12	0	—12
New Jersey	7	7		7	7	
Delaware	3	3		3	3	
Pennsylvania	1	7	+ 6	2	7	+ 5
Maryland	7	5	— 2	4	5	+ 1
Virginia	1	0	— 1	1	0	— 1
North Carolina	1	4	+ 3	1	4	+ 3
South Carolina	0	0		8	0	— 8
Georgia	0	0		0	0	
Kentucky	0	0		0	0	
Tennessee	0	0		0	0	
Totals	71	65	— 6	59	64	+ 5

NOTE: Aside from the 12 electoral votes of New York, John Adams actually gained 6 votes in the election of 1800, above his total in 1796. It was the change in New York's votes from Federalist to Democratic-Republican that made possible the victory of the new party in the election of 1800.

ELECTORAL VOTES FOR JEFFERSON AND BURR

U. S. ELECTIONS OF 1796 AND 1800

STATE	THOMAS JEFFERSON			AARON BURR		
	1796	1800	CHANGE	1796	1800	CHANGE
New Hampshire	0	0		0	0	
Vermont	0	0		0	0	
Massachusetts	0	0		0	0	
Rhode Island	0	0		0	0	
Connecticut	0	0		0	0	
New York	0	12	+12	0	12	+12
New Jersey	0	0		0	0	
Delaware	0	0		0	0	
Pennsylvania	14	8	− 6	13	8	− 5
Maryland	4	5	+ 1	3	5	+ 2
Virginia	20	21	+ 1	1	21	+20
North Carolina	11	8	− 3	6	8	+ 2
South Carolina	8	8		0	8	+ 8
Georgia	4	4		0	4	+ 4
Kentucky	4	4		4	4	
Tennessee	3	3		3	3	
Totals	68	73	+ 5	30	73	+43

NOTE: The distribution of second-place votes in the election of 1796 clearly indicates Jefferson's failure to give proper support to Burr after Burr had been selected as the Democratic-Republican candidate for Vice President. As a result, Burr requested such support in 1800, and there was a tie vote in the Electoral College, with both Jefferson and Burr receiving 73 votes.

APPENDIX B

"The Martlings"

IN THE early days of the Republic there stood at the corner of Nassau and George streets in New York City a one-story frame building known as Martling's Tavern. The proprietor was Abraham Martling. The main room was known as The Long Room, and it was here that the political supporters of Colonel Aaron Burr were accustomed to gather. Usually these gatherings were opportunistic affairs, but on some occasions there were formal meetings. Among the men who were in this group were Matthew Davis, William Van Ness, John Greenwood, John Swartwout, Samuel Swartwout, Robert Swartwout, and others. Practically all of them (but not Colonel Burr) were members of the Society of St. Tammany, or the Columbian Order. Often, because of their meeting place, they were called "The Martlings" or "Martling Men." Theodosia, remembering her Latin and her Roman history, called them "The Tenth Legion."

This group formed the nucleus of the Burr political machine in the election of 1800. It made use of certain devices which were then new but which have been used in American politics ever since that eventful contest. A card index of the registered voters was prepared and used. Gifts to the Republican campaign fund, in specified amounts, were "suggested" and solicited. A list of speakers was made, and they were assigned to address certain groups. Meetings of voters were held in each precinct and ward. Handbills were printed, and party workers were assigned the task of distributing them from door to door. And, of course, the property qualification for voters had been overcome by Colonel Burr's people through the process of the joint ownership of land.

As a result of these various measures, New York City and New York State were won for the new Republican party in 1800, although the Federalists had carried the city and the state for John Jay as Governor only one year previously.

APPENDIX C

Selected References and Source Materials

AT THE end of each chapter in this study, certain books have been cited. With very few exceptions, these reference books constitute only secondary sources of information concerning the life and career of Colonel Aaron Burr. The exceptions, which do constitute primary sources of information, are these: the collection of letters edited by Mark Van Doren, the *Annals of Congress, Senator Plumer's Memorandum, The Private Journal of Aaron Burr* (the two editions, Davis and Bixby), the Reed and Williams book, *The Case of Aaron Burr*, and the Syrett and Cooke book, *Interview in Weehawken*.

As has been mentioned in the text, there were two unfortunate events that resulted in the loss of irreplaceable collections of original documents bearing upon Colonel Aaron Burr's life and career: the wreck of the ship on which Theodosia was a passenger, en route from Georgetown to New York City on January 1, 1813, and the burning of various letters and other documents by Matthew L. Davis immediately after Colonel Burr's death on September 14, 1836. Theodosia had with her, on her ill-fated journey, some ten or twelve boxes of documents that her father had left in her care when he went to Europe in 1808, as well as much of the correspondence that had passed between them during the four years that he was out of the United States.

In spite of these losses, there still remain quite a number of

original letters, legal documents, and other papers that constitute the original sources of information, now available, concerning Colonel Aaron Burr. Unfortunately, these materials are
widely scattered. Many of them will be found in the following
libraries:

The Library of Congress, Washington, D.C.
The National Archives, Washington, D.C.
The libraries of the following Universities:

Princeton University, Princeton, New Jersey
Columbia University, New York City
Yale University, New Haven, Connecticut
Rutgers University, New Brunswick, New Jersey
The University of Chicago, Chicago, Illinois

The Massachusetts Historical Society
The New Jersey Historical Society
The New York Historical Society
The Pennsylvania Historical Society
The New York City Public Library
The Chase Manhattan Bank, New York City